IDENTIFYING CHRISTIANITY

DEMYTHOLOGIZING CHRISTIANITY

IDENTIFYING CHRISTIANITY

by René Marlé

Translated by Sister Jeanne Marie Lyons, M.M.

232. 01
MA

ABBEY PRESS
ST. MEINRAD, INDIANA 47577
1975

Identifying Christianity, the English translation of *La singularité chrétienne,* is published by contract with the original publisher, Casterman, Tournai, Belgium.

Scripture quotations are from *The Jerusalem Bible,* copyright © 1966 by Darton, Longman & Todd, Ltd. and Doubleday and Company, Inc. Used by permission of the publisher.

Contents

PART II: Within the Realm of Figures

Preface

SHOULD IT BE TRUE THAT THE CHRISTIAN FAITH NO LONGER
has anything specific, anything original, to witness to the
world, there would be nothing left for us to do but pronounce it dead.

We are not doing that. And yet, what Christianity does
specifically represent or contribute seems to be more and
more in question. On every level of life, Christians are
searching for their identity. On the personal plane, they
ask themselves what really distinguishes them from so many
of their contemporaries with whom they share the same
concerns, undergo the same trials, and live through the
same struggles. On the social plane, they question whether,
besides the great ideals about which almost the whole world
can agree, their Church has something special to offer in
the concrete work of building up the world. She means to
collaborate but does so as carrying on one of many undertakings.

If we remain persuaded in principle that the Christian
faith has a specific contribution to make, we often hesitate
as to just what it is and how it is to be offered. Does it
belong to the order of knowledge? For example, does the
faith answer questions for us which would otherwise remain unanswered? Has it to do above all with the ethical

order, with defining new demands, with giving us increased strength to fulfill moral obligations? Or does the faith rather serve us by enhancing the quasi-esthetic order, lending dignity to the celebration of events common to all men —birth, love, suffering, and death . . . ?

The present work has no intention of dealing fully with all these questions. It proposes once more to raise the problem as to just what it is that gives Christianity its specific character. It begins by considering some currents of research which have dominated theology since the Second World War. These theological trends clearly do not touch the entire life of all the churches. However, the way they have been echoed among us justifies considering them as symptomatic of a certain state of Christian consciousness. It does seem that all of them pose a problem which more or less preoccupies all believers: has Christianity something specific to offer me which it alone can give? They may state this in different ways, but all do so in a form that is particularly apt for in-depth study. The present work considers this aspect of them.

However, it will not be restricted to simply stating the question but, in connection with each position examined, will attempt to define under just what conditions the ever threatened but still recognizable face of Christianity can be preserved. In the second and more directly constructive part of the book greater consideration will be given to just what serves as a basis for the specificity of Christianity: the organic bond between the work of God and human history. There then follows an examination of the principal "patterns" which give the faith its structure and vitality so that it becomes a principle of original experience and judgment.

This essay makes no pretense of throwing light on all the searching, questioning and striving of contemporary Christianity, which can certainly be appropriately called "Christianity on the move." With it, I should like at least to do my part in making apparent what is at stake in some of the ongoing debates and, above all, to help those who seek their Christian identity to discern the irreducible object of Christian faith.

PART ONE

IS CHRISTIANITY BECOMING FACELESS?

CHAPTER 1

What Is Demythologizing?

IN THE FIELD OF THEOLOGY, THE YEARS FOLLOWING THE
Second World War were dominated by the problem of
demythologizing. Brought to the fore by Rudolf Bultmann,
it almost immediately became the subject of passionate debate in German Protestant theology and soon theologians
all over the world and of all denominations were devoting
their attention to it, some with sympathy, some with dis-
quiet, some with hostility. Later replaced by other sub-
jects of discussion, it still continues to preoccupy many
faithful and responsible people in the churches.

The intention here is not to approach the subject in all
its different aspects but, taking the project of demythologizing as a whole, to reveal it as one instance of a continuing trend to detach Christian faith from all its concrete
historical expressions.[1]

The Bultmannian Undertaking

Bultmann undertook to accomplish a task that was in
itself quite simple. It is based upon the recognition of the
distance separating the world in which the biblical writings, particularly the New Testament, were conceived and
put into writing and the world of the twentieth century in

which we live, feel, and think. Bultmann characterizes the difference between them as the opposition between a world of myth and a world with ideas irrevocably formed by science and technology. In the world of myth the divine continually intervened in nature and found no difficulty in mingling in the history of the world and of men. The contemporary world belongs to the order of sensible experience and temporal action and obeys its laws. The world of the twentieth-century man does not necessarily exclude reference to another reality outside these structural laws but, for it, such a reality could not be perceived on the same level or envisaged from the same standpoint. The man of the twentieth century has received a strictly scientific education; and, according to Bultmann, his faith as well as his knowledge of the world can only gain from that fact.

For, if it is true that the New Testament has reference to a mythical image of the world, that does not of itself make the New Testament outdated. Its object is not, in fact, to give us a cosmology but to have us listen to a message only accidentally formulated within a mythical framework. The purpose of demythologizing, consequently, has no other end than to free this message from the representative apparatus in which it has been brought to us so that it may be expressed in its ever living actuality. Demythologizing is only the negative side of an essentially positive undertaking, the "existential interpretation" of the message so that, unencumbered, its significance for life reaches the people to whom it is addressed.

Now man's existence is essentially a "historical" existence, that is, it is always realized in the actuality of a "decision" which, abandoning a dead past (or a past conceived as such), projects itself into a future that it really causes to come to pass. Only by taking this historicity into consideration is it possible to formulate a message which gets through to man's **reality.**

In fact, historicity is only fully realized in response to the message. Such at least is what the New Testament itself declares. For, as long as it has not been heard, man is invincibly closed up within his own self-sufficiency, which he only reinforces when doing his utmost to break through it, for self-sufficiency blinds a man and reduces him to powerlessness since it makes him incapable of responding to the Word that comes to denounce and pardon it and so free a man from its hold. The Word is, in fact, the one real new and extraordinary "given." It comes to announce that "where man cannot act, God acts, and has acted, for him." Such is the heart of the New Testament message, the gospel, the good news of salvation that restores man to his real being and opens up life to him.

Bultmann rejects what seems to him dependence upon mythological representations that are no longer acceptable and seeks to interpret the New Testament kerygma within the structures of human existence. He does not mean to reduce the Christian message to some kind of rational discourse on man or the world, which would take away the freshness of the Gospel and the originality of biblical faith. On the contrary, he intends to emphasize the character of the Word of God as a contingent happening. This Word has become a reality of our world in what he calls the Christ-event as it is actualized here and now.

It is true that, in order to "make us a part of" it, the Word has not left off referring to mythological representatives—the preexistence of a "Son of God," who, "when the time was accomplished," became a man, was born of a virgin, paid the debt for our sins by his blood, is now seated at the right hand of God before returning to pronounce the last judgment. . . . But, in Bultmann's thought, these representatives, although expressed in the language of the times, have definitely in view only the "eschatological,"

that is, the final and absolute significance and import of the
Christ-event in the order of salvation.

Bultmann defines Christian faith in relation to an event
which, on the plane of perceptible history, is reduced to its
pure factuality (what is called the *Dass,* the pure fact that
it has taken place), and to a universal but apparently entirely abstract signification of that event. Its structure is an
absolute "paradox." This view alone, he tells us, does
justice to the fundamental Johannine statement, "The Word
has become flesh," by giving its full weight to each word.
It alone gives full value to the Pauline theme of the folly
of the cross.

The paradoxical structure of the faith does not lead the
believer to have any less respect for the laws of the world
or the indefeasible demands of reason, whether on the
theoretical or on the practical level, since the significance
invested in the Christ-event is not a palpable notification
but is proclaimed and received "in spite of" everything that
it manifests to eyes of flesh. For the faith, this temporal
manifestation has not, as such, any more content than a
mathematical point and anything that can be added to it at
this level appertains to natural knowledge, without any import for salvation.

Yet, for all that, the world is not left to itself. Around
the pivotal point constituting the "fact" of Christ and in the
light of the Word which affirms its eschatological import, a
radical change in its meaning takes place. All is at once
the same and different, just as the sinner remains a sinner
on earth and yet, in God, is already justified by his faith.
In him an infinite distance exists between what is and what
seems. As Bultmann has a predilection for quoting, he is in
the world as not being of it (see 1 Cor 7:29-35). Just as
the pitifully inadequate word of the Church, following upon
the equally human word of the biblical authors and the
scandal of the cross, is perceived by a believer as a salva-

tion event, so each new day that dawns becomes, within the secret of his apparently unchanged existence, a reflection of God's glory.

The "Scandal" of the Faith

It is impossible and unjust to relegate Bultmann to the ranks of the liberalists, basically preoccupied with stripping away the distinctive character of Christian faith to make it more acceptable to people. Indeed, his concern is rather to remove false obstacles, those which a man can come to think that, if need be, he can surmount by fettering his energies, by doing violence to his greatest needs, those of light and truth, by mortifying his noblest faculties for motives and by means always suspect. But Bultmann avoids false paths only to highlight the real "scandal": salvation bound up with a man who is truly man and offered up on a cross. Only by the power of God, who is affirmed by faith, can it be done. There is no other victory to be gained over the world: "This is the victory over the world—our faith" (1 Jn 5:4).

If the power of God alone can, through faith, triumph over the world and, by condemning it, save it, this is because man is at root a sinner. Those for whom Bultmann's theology is only a revived form of natural rationalism should not fail to notice the decisive place it accords to the consideration of sin: from the beginning sin affects the whole being of man and his every enterprise. To Bultmann's way of thinking, recognition of sin and its acknowledgment mark the decisive cleavage between the concept of man expressed in the New Testament and that underlying every philosophic venture and all natural mysticism. By placing man directly under the judgment of God, the New Testament clearly manifests his absolutely fallen state. His spontaneous effort is to escape judgment in order to become himself, to attain by his own powers his true being,

in a word, to give himself salvation. Man's fallenness finds
expression even at the highest point of the efforts he makes
to surmount it. Here he pushes his pretentiousness, his self-
glorification, his *kauchesis,* in the New Testament, to the
limit. Pride raises man up in a way as foolish as it is
fatal, to stand up to the face of God.

Furthermore, something entirely new has to enter in here
for the issue to reach this really desperate situation. This
something absolutely new is the "fact" of Christ alluded to
earlier. Upon it the universe of the believer balances. From
this point of view too Christianity as defined by Bultmann
is marked by a constitutive specificity. It does not belong
to the order of general ideas. It is deeply rooted in history
and refers at every moment to the irreducible event of its
starting point.

A Description "at the Limit"

What can cause difficulty is the exiguous and in some
sense evanescent character of this starting point. It affects
the whole concept of the historical evolution of Christian
realities.

Bultmann has insisted, time and time again, that Christianity cannot be reduced to a system of ideas. All the
notions in the New Testament which serve to formulate
it are found or can be found elsewhere. What constitutes
Christianity is the effective realization and the actual affirmation of something beyond ideas: the affirmation and
realization of the fact that God is indeed here right now,
hic et nunc, and for me; that His pardon is spoken and His
grace is given; that a new relationship is established between my Creator and Savior, and me. Bultmann points
out that this is true of Jesus' preaching: "What he says, he
does not say as something not heard before. But *that* he
says it, that he is saying it *now,* is the decisive event; and
the saying changes the situation for all who hear him into

a new and decisive situation."[2]

Bultmann thinks that he can thus work *at the limit* of objectivity, there where the word, and even the person, become pure act, without constituent content. We know that at one time Barth, in an attempt to express the relationship between the Word of God and the world, used the comparison of the tangent that meets the circumference only at a point without ever becoming merged with it, unless "at the limit." This comparison, it seems, could equally well serve to interpret Bultmann's conception of how the work of God (what he would call the eschatological realities) relates to the historical realities of the world. A point that should be insisted upon is that he does not attempt, in any true sense of the word, to extract a nontemporal "essence" out of Christianity, as Harnack, for example, tried to do. He works rather, I venture to say, by using the language of mathematics to establish the differential law of its constitution.

This law, which comprises an indisputable part of truth, has the advantage of integrating the movement of divine salvation and therefore, in principle, of accounting for its effectiveness. It has the drawback of remaining abstract, of staying on the level of "principle." Like a graph or a formula, it can at the very most "represent" the general structure of time and space, of corporeality and of existence, within which the work of Christian salvation is accomplished. It does not disclose their actual extension and weight. And the danger is great, if not to say fatal, that a blow is thus dealt to the realism involved in biblical faith.

A Break between "the Signifying" and the "Signified"

This theology is attractive because it is exact and systematic. However, its deficiencies soon become apparent at every level. We will only enumerate the principal ones. They first appear in the oversimplified way in which

Bultmann establishes a break between the "mythical" language of biblical writings and their meaning at the level of existence. As already remarked, he understands the different mythical representations as giving the same definitive, universal, and abstract signification, the "eschatological" import—that is, the final and absolute meaning of the Christ-event. As Paul Ricoeur rightly observes in his brilliant introduction to the French translation of Bultmann's little book *Jesus,* the author's hermeneutical principles fail to take into account (although his exegetical practice does not) an essential moment in any faithful interpretation: the focusing on the content and meaning of the text itself before becoming preoccupied with its actual, practical application to personal existence. The moment of attention to "the given" is, with Bultmann, short-circuited by his pursuit of its direct, immediate effect on real action, real involvement, and real life. The ultrapersonalism governing this theology should, according to Ricoeur, be corrected and completed by some points from the structuralist school of thought which, on the contrary, comes to a stop with the internal, immanent structuring of sense elements.[3]

A correction and completion of this kind would make possible a more exact interpretation and, as a result, a far different reading of the formulas and representations through which Christian truth is proposed to us. At the present time, in fact, ethnology, linguistics, phenomenology, and the history of religions have all thrown light upon the astonishingly revealing power of myths and of symbolic language in general. "It is the power and the mission of images," writes Mircea Eliade, "to *show* all that remains refractory to the concept...."[4] And we know Ricoeur's perceptive and frequently repeated formula: symbols and myths "make us think."

We need not then see in the language of imagery used in the Bible the weakness of minds unable to reach the

conceptual level or which, having attained it, would have
to retreat immediately to the plane of the existent, even
when making a response to a personal summons. If there
be weakness, it is the weakness of a love which, in order
to speak with us, has taken on all our human ways. And
if there are representations in the biblical writings which
derive from the times when they were conceived and com-
posed, they testify to God's fidelity in dealing with our
human condition. We can seek to understand them aright
and to interpret them correctly by bringing out their full
meaning, but all the while we have to be on our guard not
to break the bond which binds them to the weight of time
and the density of flesh. For they refer not just to an existential significance, an act of "summoning," but also to a
concrete figure, the Incarnate Word, not as just "an event,"
a word which in and by its very proclamation would yield
up its whole substance, but "the image of the invisible
God" (Col 1:15). Looked at in this way, the task of
theology, rooted as it should be in the biblical word, could
not rightly be said to be to "demythologize" the Bible by
detaching an existential signification from its body of expression. It is rather to gain greater possession of the revealing discourse inaugurated by the Word of God made
flesh, being careful to respect it and yet without fear of
developing it.

Disembodying the Body

In the oversimplified and too hasty treatment which
Bultmann accords the mythical or so-called mythical data
met with in the New Testament, we have already come
upon another area where the deficiencies of his proposed
theology make themselves plain. This is Christology and
especially everything that has to do with the doctrine concerning Christ's body, which Bultmann is content to include
among the Gnostic themes to be found in the New Testa-

ment. As we are to return to the christological problem in the following chapter, the preceding brief remarks might suffice at this juncture. On the other hand, in close connection with what has been said about breaking the organic bond uniting the meaning of the biblical message to its body of expression, it must be pointed out how impossible it is for Bultmannian theology to give significance to the body of man and to all in which the body concurs for the realization of existence and particularly believing existence. For Bultmann, human existence is completely defined by its "historicity" in the sense given earlier. It is expressed essentially in an upsurge of pure freedom, self-released at a *hic et nunc* encounter with the word. The word is itself "event" and, by summoning a man, requires him "to decide."

Does this not mean forgetting or ignoring the constitutive role of those fundamental relationships within which the whole of human existence is realized—relationships of generation, of production, and of consummation? If it is true that, in the action of "decision" which constitutes a response of faith, our past recedes under the creative radiance of the future so that it becomes transfigured into it, does this act of decision ever assume the absolute character attributed to it by Bultmann? Is not our spiritual destiny worked out through a sequence of concrete decisions linked to a limited scheme of things? And while our decisions do not cease to represent a creative and evolving process, are they not also woven into the temporal *continuum,* the work of revelation and salvation in the past as well as the present?

To recall that our human existence is actualized in a body within the opaque sphere of time means recalling too that, even in the case of faith, it is not possible to reduce it to an instantaneous act of absolute response given in full enlightenment to the completely luminous Word of God. Faith is a journeying (2 Cor 5:7). During it we see only "a dim reflection in a mirror" (1 Cor 13:12). Faith is engaged in a struggle wherein clear consciousness acts in concert with the subtle play of the unconscious buried in the depths of our past and of our flesh. Bultmann bases himself on St. Paul to formulate "eschatological faith" as he understands it, that is, as situated at the limit of the world and of time. Yet St. Paul shows in many places and interprets eloquently the meaning of a destiny by which we mature while bearing the weight of the flesh and of history. It is not only "the entire creation" that "has been groaning in one great act of giving birth." We too, "all of us who possess the firstfruits of the Spirit . . . groan inwardly as we wait for our bodies to be set free" (Rom 8:22-23).

Man's work is one of the areas in which this "giving birth," this "being set free," takes place. It is significant that it receives hardly any consideration in Bultmann's anthropology and, consequently, in the existential interpretation of the Christian message which he gives us. The principal, if not the only, comment which he makes about work concerns the excessive value placed upon it in our contemporary civilization, which is becoming more and more incapable of appreciating the gratuitous activities of the spirit. Bultmann's man has no dirt on his hands but, as in Peguy's view of Kantianism, he has no hands.

Christian tradition has always seen in both work and suffering the hidden source for maturing men and the great crucible in which holiness is forged. Bultmann gives scarcely any value to suffering. He does know, it is true, that "not only actions but human sufferings too belong to history" and can find meaning there. But if that is possible, he tells us, it is because "in a certain sense, they are also actions to the extent that they are reactions." It is surely correct that as soon as suffering becomes conscious, some reaction on the part of the sufferer is implied. But does

not the real mystery of suffering lie in the opacity which
it guards just when we try to discover its meaning and in
that irreducible obscurity which the man invested with it
himself encounters? And is it not Christian faith which reveals to us the sovereign power of this night, the disconcerting fruitfulness of this *passion*? Is it not just here that
we are asked to acknowledge the appeals of a will alien to
our recalcitrant flesh and heart, to recognize the intrusion
of the unknown, the wholly other, the altogether new?

Taking into account Bultmann's views cited here, it is
not surprising that he finds it difficult to accord the sacraments a value properly their own since their role is to
actualize for the participation of the faithful the *acta et
passa Christi in carne,* what Christ did and suffered in the
flesh. Bultmann interprets these *acta et passa* simply as
verba visibilia, visible words. And visible words they certainly are. However, for him their "visibility" serves only
to risk further perversion. Does not the sensible character
of the sacraments rather remind us that the "words" which
they express (for they should, let it be said again, speak
as much as possible) are not, however, just "words." They
are words grafted into the reality of an existence; they are
charged with, penetrated by, flesh and blood. That is why
they are fitting to regenerate Christians in body as well as
spirit, that is, in their whole time-bound existence. Anyone who understands this need not see the maxim of St.
Ignatius of Antioch that the Eucharist is a *pharmacon
athansiae,* a remedy for eternity, as Bultmann does. He
views it as the acme of mythical thought. It is rather a con-
densed translation of the Johannine discourse on the bread
of life: "Anyone who does eat my flesh and drink my blood
has eternal life, and I will raise him up on the last day"
(Jn 6:54).

Revelation without Historical Development

The sacraments—we will treat them later—ensure that

the lived Christian faith is firmly rooted in history. Interpreting them in a minimizing, not to say disparaging, way goes along quite naturally with Bultmann's disregard of the historical *development* of the Word of revelation. He formally rejects even the idea of it. This is the final point of view that will be dealt with in order to point out its significant deficiencies. These have something to teach us.

For Bultmann, the idea of a *paideia,* a divine pedagogy, is a specifically Greek notion, foreign to biblical thinking. The Word of God can only merge momentarily with the world and with a human being. Their capacity to receive it is given essentially in the "contradiction" to it which they represent.

This conception is expressed in an unusual interpretation of the meaning of the Old Testament for Christian faith. Rejecting allegorical interpretations and those originating in the consideration of "the history of salvation," Bultmann retains just one, based on certain propositions developed by St. Paul in relation to the Law: he sees the Old Testament as an instrument for witnessing to the vain efforts of man to acquire the grace of God by his own efforts; he sees it as a continual reminder of an order which the Gospel came to bring to an end. If it prepares for the gift of God accomplished in Jesus Christ, it is only by way of contrast and opposition. Man can have prophetic value only through the failure of his own resources, only by recognizing the impossibility of entering, during his intraworldly history, into direct possession of God, of identifying his intraworldly history with the action of God.[5]

Nevertheless, is not intraworldly history in itself, and particularly so in Jesus Christ, the bearer of God's action and salvation? And can the history of Jesus Christ be separated from the history of the people to whom He belongs? Then, too, in Christian tradition, the Old Testament has never served simply as a means of recalling the antithesis between the Law and the Gospel. Tradition has always recognized the fabric of which the Gospel has been made.[6] Indeed Bultmann has seen that the passage from the Old Testament to the New expresses in some way the very movement of our faith. But this movement on the level of faith comes to pass only because it is founded on what has first taken place in the mystery of Christ's life, death and resurrection: the consummate revelation of God's fidelity and the fulfillment of all that He has promised. If we can then, as Bultmann concedes, reread the Old Testament by hearing it speak of Jesus, it is not just because any reality whatsoever can, after the event, function in accord with the faith expressed by those who already believe; it is primarily and essentially because Jesus Himself has assimilated it to Himself, after having in some way taken it into His body of flesh, and having laid bare its mysterious meaning when He delivered up that body on the cross and poured out His Spirit upon our world.

The Old Testament is needed to verify that the Word of God is truly rooted in history. This truth, in its turn, defines the status of a faith which, as Dietrich Bonhoeffer has written, sees the final realities through realities that are "before the last," and attains the invisible goods to which it is ordered only by remaining faithful to the visible things which the Spirit of God does not absorb but does transfigure.

Faith responds to God in a way that is consonant with God's own fidelity. His promises are not accomplished only in the proclamation of an eschatological *Now* bound up with the manifestation of Jesus but, more fundamentally, in the reality of His body, born of a woman of our race and delivered up on the cross to become the principle of a whole new creation.

We have not attempted to review in the preceding pages everything that has been said or could be said about the problem of demythologizing; still less, to take up again a comprehensive exposition and discussion of Bultmann's thought. What was proposed was simply, through reference to a particularly representative theme of recent theological research, to bring to the surface the symptoms of a whole orientation to which attention should be called because it is serious, important, and apparently also fraught with some dangers. These are not presented as completely identical with those put forward in anti-Bultmann polemics. Those have been chiefly concerned with his critical skepticism and the reductive character of his exegesis. Without ruling out the possibility of carrying the argument in that direction—we are going to return to it in the following chapter —it seems to us that it is within theological perspectives as such, on the level of a whole interpretation of Christian faith, that the debate ought to be conducted. The present study is directly concerned with pursuing the subject on that plane.

Under the circumstances, the importance of such a confrontation relates to a theological project undertaken to prevent Christianity from being reduced to an abstract system of ideas and to bind it to the unique event of Jesus Christ and the Word emanating from him. However, the smallness of this event, when detached from what has been called its body expression, involves, in spite of the intentions with which the theology was begun, leaving behind the realm of faith, that is, of a progressive advance oriented to the light within a mystery, which defines the place of our believing existence and never ceases to inform it at all levels without, however, being exhausted in that which it actualizes.

What Bultmann does not take into account, especially in his project of demythologizing and existential interpretation, is both the whole character of this mystery and the depth to which, according to biblical revelation, it penetrates the history and existence of men to form them and give them,

while living as they do within the very womb of the world,
a special "look" all their own.

CHAPTER 2

Is the Historical Jesus
Foreign to Faith?

THE PROBLEM OF DEMYTHOLOGIZING WAS PARTICULARLY
predominant during the first ten years following the Second
World War. Without dropping out of public notice since,
it has been partly replaced by the problem of "the historical
Jesus."

The two problems are not unrelated. Moreover, they
originated in the work of the same author. The problem
of the historical Jesus forms part of the framework of the
general discussion of Bultmann's work. Therefore, it is not
surprising that the same fundamental bent shows up here
and arouses the same critical reaction on my part. The
problem of demythologizing dealt with the relationship of
the supposedly mythical elements of the New Testament to
the kerygma, to the act of the Word expressed through them.
The problem of the historical Jesus has to do with the relationship of historical data concerning Jesus to the Christ
confessed in faith as "the eschatological event of salvation."

In any event, it is under the fundamental aspect of the
historical Jesus that I want to view demythologizing, making no pretence of exhausting all that could be said on
either subject.[1]

A Glance at History

Like many others, the problem of Jesus has taken on
new life as critical methods have come into general use.
Up until then the fundamental trust accorded the documents telling us of Jesus led us, at least in the Christian
world, to accept Him without question as a historical figure
and a witness of divine revelation. Beginning with the
eighteenth century, doubt as to the historical value of the
sources of faith became widespread, as we know. Reimarus
(1694-1768) elaborated an entire interpretation of the
Gospels on the basis that they were fraudulent.

Critical work, however, has not led only to harmful
views. Many who devoted themselves to it considered it
rather as a matter of returning to the solid ground of history, considered as the one possible basis for an enlightened
faith as opposed to dogma—including first and foremost
that of the New Testament authors—assimilated more or
less arbitrarily. It was the era of "lives of Jesus."

At the beginning of our century, Albert Schweitzer
described the history and the results of *The Quest for the
Historical Jesus,*[2] according to the title of his scholarly
thesis. The account which he gave amounted to a report
of appalling failure. The Jesus brought to light by different
authors reflected in a disturbing way the ideal (whether
humanitarian or social or religious) of each one who
claimed to be objectively reconstructing his traits.

By continually pushing critical skepticism farther and
farther, rationalist positivism, which usually dominated the
"lives of Jesus" enterprise, opened up the way to fideism.
In a work destined to become famous and having an aston-
ishing timeliness at present, *The So-Called Historical Jesus
and the Historical Biblical Christ,* Martin Kahler in 1892
had already set himself to show that "the historical Jesus
of modern authors conceals from us the living Christ of the
Bible."[3] From that period on, however, the documents of

primitive Christianity were thought to convey nothing but their faith. Or, at least, it was judged impossible to look beyond their testimony and find there a historical reality to which their faith was only a response. Such is, we know, the orientation of exegesis inspired by *Formgeschichte,* "the history of forms," in its beginnings. It led to considering the encounter with the word of God in faith as a meeting of two subjectivities, without any objective elements.

Bultmann has clearly gone the farthest along this route, After his *History of the Synoptic Tradition,*[4] one of the foundation stones of the "history of forms" method, it led him in 1926 to undertake the writing of his *Jesus.*[5] Since then he has not given up working out the theory implied in these first works. The positions he has taken have proved the starting point for the recent controversy concerning the historical Jesus.

Bultmann's Position

In the introduction to his *Jesus,* Bultmann states, "I do indeed think that we can know almost nothing concerning the life and personality of Jesus, since the early Christian sources show no interest in either, are moreover fragmentary and often legendary; and other sources about Jesus do not exist."[6]

This statement, more than any other perhaps, created anxiety and scandal. Many saw in its "hypercriticism" the ruin of faith. Bultmann is not of the same mind and declares that his critical radicalism has left his own faith undisturbed. In fact, according to him, if this ignorance, these unresolvable uncertainties can upset a historian, they cannot affect either a believer or a theologian. For faith, which the theologian endeavors to express, cannot be grounded on the purely human attempts and results of history or any other science whatsoever. Bultmann recalls that St. Paul was able to build up his whole Gospel and his

entire theology without actually referring to the human
existence of Jesus; at the very most, he affirms the *Dass,*
the simple reality of His human being, the pure fact that
He has been in our world. This is, in particular, the whole
content of Gal 4:4: "born of a woman, born a subject of
the Law"; and Paul has put still greater emphasis on the
vanity of knowing Christ "according to the flesh" (2 Cor
5:16), interpreted by Bultmann as knowledge of the historical Jesus obtained through the natural processes of experience and investigation.

So, in his *Theology of the New Testament,*[7] Bultmann
places the preaching of Jesus among the "presuppositions"
of this theology. According to him, it cannot, in fact, be
an immediate part of it. For Christian faith, he explains,
begins only when he who preached has himself become an
object of preaching, when he has been proclaimed as "God's
eschatological act." The theology of the New Testament
is an account of the faith expressed in this preaching.

For the same reason, when Bultmann deals with the
problem of the messianic consciousness of Jesus, he says
that he concurs with Wrede's thesis that messiahship was
attributed to Jesus by Christians after His resurrection and
at that time artificially introduced into the account of His
public life by the evangelists, especially Mark. However,
he views this question, no matter how interesting it may be
in itself, as belonging to scientific investigation and having
no importance for a believer.[8]

> Rather, the acknowledgement of Jesus as the one in
> whom God's word decisively encounters man, what-
> ever title be given to him—"Messias (Christ)," "Son
> of Man," "Lord"—is a pure act of faith independent
> of the answer to the historical question whether or
> not Jesus considered himself the Messiah. Only the
> historian can answer this question—as far as it can

be answered at all—and faith, being a personal decision, cannot be dependent upon a historian's labor.[9]

Reactions within the Bultmannian School

These specific positions were challenged and passionately disputed over the years 1952-1953. The first to contest Bultmann's thesis on this subject were his own pupils, especially one of the best known, Ernst Käsemann. At the time of the annual reunion for former students of Marburg in 1952, Käsemann made the problem of the historical Jesus the subject of a distinguished conference.[10] The debate initiated at that time was to continue for years. It touches on a matter of such importance that it cannot be said to be definitively closed even now.

Käsemann first stated that his master's skepticism about having any knowledge of the historical Jesus seemed to him exaggerated, and that "the theological consequences of his skepticism" were, to his mind, "dangerous." He called attention to the fact that developments in this area among Bultmann's pupils were coming about through the progress made by exegesis since the time of the earliest works of the "history of forms." During this progress, the historical "givens" about Jesus that are relatively certain have been pointed up more sharply and, at least as regards the Synoptics, their historical purpose, along with their kerygmatic objectives, has been more clearly recognized. No doubt remains, he explained, that it is no longer possible for us to reconstruct with any certainty a complete life of Jesus. However, "resignation and skepticism" could not constitute the final say of any serious inquiry. "In the Synoptic tradition there are elements," he said, "which a historian simply has to recognize as authentic, if he wants to remain a historian."

Furthermore, an objective consideration of the New Testament "givens" forces us to recognize that, if the first

Christian generation "was convinced that the earthly Jesus could only be understood from the basis of Easter, it is equally true that Easter cannot be adequately comprehended if the earthly Jesus is made an abstraction."[11] Besides, the purpose directing the formulation and writing of the Gospels, besides the other New Testament writings, testifies to the importance that Christian faith, from its beginnings, has placed on the figure of the Jesus of history.

But it is also for reasons of reflection and of principle that Käsemann and some other exegetes of his generation objected to the radical break introduced by Bultmann between the Jesus of history and the Christ of the kerygma. The moment represented by historical knowledge assures the objectivity, that is, the *extra nos* character of salvation. Without this basic preliminary to faith, faith is in danger of having no other foundation than itself, of being, in other words, the product of human will, if not an act of abdication before the authority of a church commanding belief. Bultmann insists that faith cannot rest on a human enterprise, such as historical investigations. But as Gerhard Ebeling, another of Bultmann's disciples, remarks, history is not the only reality to which a man can become wedded. The spirit, that transcendent power by which a man can claim to be possessed, is equally capable of degenerating into a pretext for proud self-assertion, as St. Paul reminded the enlightened ones of Corinth. And if the Word of God is not intrinsically qualified by Him who is at the same time its message and its messenger, it loses any power to arouse us to respond, to decide. Ebeling goes on to say that he feels himself stirred to decision by other histories of ideas and that the preaching exercising the greatest fascination over the majority of people today is not Christ's but Marx's.

Beginning with these fundamental considerations, Bultmann's critical pupils set themselves to show the essential continuity between the manifestation of Jesus, His "posture," and the titles conferred on Him by the kerygma, a point of view developed by Ernst Fuchs, among others. They placed even more emphasis on the point that Jesus is the foundation of the kerygma, contained in germ, *in nuce,* within His "I," so that it is possible for us to see in Jesus, according to the formula in the Epistle to the Hebrews, the author and finisher of our faith (Heb 12:2), a perspective developed with predilection by Gerhard Ebeling. Bultmann, for his part, sees the line followed by his students as a regrettable reversion to the positions taken by nineteenth-century liberal theology.

Other Voices, Other Views

Many theologians and exegetes whose works do not follow in Bultmann's wake are plainly no less categorical in their rejection of a theology that relegates the Jesus of history to a position outside the faith. It would seem to be sufficient here to cite some names and to recall some of the most important observations bearing on the subject.

In 1958, the Lutheran theologian Paul Althaus published a short work entitled "The Kerygma and the Historical Jesus" with the subtitle "A Critique of Contemporary Theology concerning the Kerygma."[12] After first refuting certain fundamental principles of Bultmann's theology, he writes:

> The character of revelation belonging to the history of Jesus is not recognized *by* reflection on the plane of historical science. On the other hand, it is not *without* it. For the Gospel deals with actions that must have happened in human history; it has "the historical" as its content and its foundation in history forms part of its credibility.[13]

Althaus takes a stand against Bultmann's exegesis of St.

Paul's statements relative to knowledge of Christ "according to the flesh": "the *kata sarka* (according to the flesh) does not have to do with the object 'Christ' but with the verb 'to know'." The kerygma, Althaus insists, relates to an event which is not identified purely and simply with it. The preaching of the Church has recourse to the testimony of those who were close to Jesus and always consists in the exposition, the tradition, of this testimony, at all times taking care to establish its authenticity, a point that the Church has never failed to consider essential. Therefore, to the reality of the *humanitas Christi,* without which there is no Christianity, corresponds a *fides humana,* which does not create a *fides divina* but serves as its presupposition. The same author explains in this connection:

> It is not enough to say that the Word of God, because it is the Word of God, has its authority in itself. That does not completely explain the *specific* authority of the apostolic preaching . . . The *historic* moment implied in this authority is not given its due worth: it must no longer be drained away from the Church's contemporary preaching. The authority for the preaching of the Church stems from the fact that the word today is an exposition of apostolic testimony.[14]

Indeed it is because of this bond with historical greatness that the authority of God really reaches us:

> The Gospel's power to draw us to believe is bound up with the fact that the kerygma includes the Gospels with their concrete image of Jesus. In the human image of Jesus we grasp the character of God, in the spiritual visage of Jesus we behold the visage of God. From the Gospels a living person looks out at us and wins our faith. The kerygma becomes first an in-

tellectual proposition, a dogma, if we do not see it filled with the living image of the Jesus of the Gospels.[15]

As a result of the absorbing interest that leads him to call to mind the presence of God's glory on the face of Christ (2 Cor 4:6), Althaus objects to the diminished character of Bultmannian Christology because of its narrow anthropological nature. "The New Testament," he emphasizes, "does not see Jesus Christ only in His relationship to us . . . but also in His relationship to the *Father.*" Likewise, in the paschal event, as it is presented to us in Scripture, it is not just a matter of faith being awakened in the soul of the believer but "also, and first of all, of the action accomplished by God in Christ." Flowing from that fact, Jesus is not revealed simply as Lord *quoad me, my* Lord, but as exercising His lordship over demon and over death, as the creator of a whole new world. "The coming of the Kingdom of God does indeed signify the salvation of man. But that God reigns is a theme with its own value. Here we are in the presence of realities that must not be forced into a narrow anthropological outlook."[16]

According to Althaus, the abstract, fleshless kerygma proposed to us by some modern theologies leads to a rule of law, of moral imperative and human decision, as if these sufficed to effect salvation. At this point the Christian economy is left behind.

In a short but illuminating study on *The Problem of the Historical Jesus,* Joachim Jeremias emphasizes the new tools that we have at our disposal when undertaking research on the Jesus of history: a highly refined literary critique; new vistas opened up by form criticism itself; new data about the era with the discovery of Qumran; and studies made on the Galilean-Aramaic dialect which Jesus must have spoken.[17] He then concludes:

> If with utmost discipline and conscientiousness we ap-
> ply the critical resources at our disposal to the study
> of the historical Jesus, the final result is always the
> same: we find ourselves confronted with God himself.
> . . . It is not as if faith were made superfluous or be-
> littled, when exegesis shows us that behind every word
> and every deed of Jesus lies his claim of authority.
> (How could faith ever become superfluous?) Indeed,
> the truth of the matter is that through the words and
> acts of Jesus at every turn the challenge to faith is
> presented."[18]

At a highly technical level, the Catholic exegete Heinz
Schürmann undertakes to show how it is possible, within
the very perspectives of form criticism, to get past agnostic
and fideist conclusions by reaching the *Sitz im Leben,* the
life situation, of the prepaschal community.[19] He states
that, in fact, there can be no question of denying the existence of a "sociological community" or, linked to it, a
"confessional continuity" in the community of the disciples.
A continuity in its kerygmatic and missionary movement
has to be admitted as well. The preaching about Christ who
died and rose again is not unrelated to the initiation which
Jesus gave to His disciples when sending them on mission.

> Using the very principles of form criticism, it can be
> shown (see Acts 1:21-26; Lk 1:2; 1 Jn 1:1-7) that
> the beginnings of the tradition of the *Logia,* the words
> of Jesus, have to be located in the prepaschal circle
> of His disciples and so in Jesus Himself. Therefore,
> by the very method of form criticism, access to "the
> historical Jesus" opens up, for "the historical Jesus"
> is Himself a constituent element in the event of tradi-
> tion—its initiator. In other words, the method of
> form criticism can deal with "the historical Jesus"
> without having, for that reason, to go outside the

domain of the history of traditions to vault into history properly speaking. For, in its beginning, history is largely a history of traditions, and inversely, the history of traditions represents history.[20]

Just as Käsemann brings out the dialectical relationship between knowledge of the earthly Jesus and knowledge of the paschal Christ that the exegete must recognize, Schürmann emphasizes that only such a relationship makes it possible to avoid the deadly literalism of Judaism on the one hand and the false spiritualism of Gnosis on the other.

> Only the *Kyrios* and the *Pneuma* really make Christian tradition just what it is. A tradition without a mandate from the *Kyrios* and unprompted by the impulse of the *Pneuma* would become a *gramma,* a letter (2 Cor 3:6), and would be at the very least akin to the rabbinical tradition. But, inversely, a tradition based exclusively on the fact of Easter and Pentecost, with no link to the historical Jesus (1 Cor 11:23) and to the prepaschal circle of His disciples, would lose the *factum historicum* and could no longer be distinguished from Gnosis.[21]

Wolfhart Pannenberg, in his *Jesus—God and Man,*[22] adopts a more systematic position. His thesis rests on the idea that Christian faith has its foundation in history. "Only when its revelatory character is not something additional to the events but, rather, is inherent in them can the events form the basis for faith."[23] To the objection that faith can find no basis in the human results of science, Pannenberg first replies that the believer can only have confidence that the reality of the event on which he has taken his stand will continue to be verified anew throughout the whole course of historical inquiry. Then he adds that faith is confidence placed in God's promises, a confidence not made superfluous but simply possible by a knowledge of them. Believing confidence that rests on a promise given with assurance leads to future fulfillment. In any case, "faith primarily has to do with what Jesus *was*. Only from that can we know what he is for us today and how proclamation about him is possible today."[24] Pannenberg is convinced that we can and ought to go beyond the testimony of the apostles to Jesus Himself by seeking to learn the relationship of the New Testament texts to the situation which they reflect and, so to say, making deductions from them. "Going back behind the apostolic kerygma to the historical Jesus is, therefore, possible. It is also necessary."[25]

Unlike Any Other—the Gospel Jesus

If it is true that, according to Althaus's formula, the faith that we live by and proclaim ought to be filled with the living image of the gospel Jesus, we must not forget the mysterious nature of that image. As we are often reminded nowadays, the gospels were not set down on the model of a police report. They are not constructed along the lines of a film documentary, and the words of Jesus are not reproduced as they would be on a tape recording. Objectivity, however, could not be better assured. We know how problematic objectivity always remains in spite of modern means of communication like photography, radio, television. Every camera shot, every recording, every account is necessarily a choice, an excision made from an always complex and inexhaustible reality. A few days after the first showing of Frederic Rossif's film on the October revolution, a critic reviewed it. Although Rossif had made his film from shots of the events at the time and then afterwards of the places where they had happened, the critic, while recognizing the undeniable interest of the project, made the point that, nevertheless, it gave the viewer a less perceptively seen and lived experience of the revolution in its living reality than, for example, S. M. Eisenstein's more or less epic—and in some details, inexact—reproduction.[26] Each reality can only be properly expressed in a literary genre suited to its nature. No matter how correct a police report may be from its own point of view, it will never express the whole reality of a human drama written up as a case. The recent decree of the Pontifical Biblical Commission on the historical truth of the Gospels, restated in substance by the Conciliar Constitution on Revelation, *Dei Verbum,* emphasizes the complex character of the genesis of the Gospels and insists on the necessity of keeping in mind the perspectives within which they were written.[27] They are compositions; each has a particular end in view. They certainly were intended to hand on to us authentically the truth about Jesus, His teaching, and His work. But they do not attempt to satisfy our curiosity about everything we would like to know, particularly whatever would be beside the point, in other words, things that would have no bearing on faith.

So we could never issue an identification card for Jesus. Everything featured on such cards, all that could be useful for police surveillance and work, remains ever unknown to us. It is not at this level, not within a sphere of this kind, that we can discover who Jesus really was and what He came to tell us and to accomplish. That is what the Gospels pass on to us not only with fidelity but also with unparalleled evocative power. So true is this that every other image of Jesus that can be proposed to us disappoints us, seems pitifully unequal to its subject. For example, when we see Jesus represented on the screen, it makes no difference with what reverence the scenario was written, with what artistry the film has been produced, or with what discrimination the actor plays his part, we never fail to say to ourselves: "But Jesus was certainly something other, something much more than that." And what gives us this conviction is the image formed in us and which, moreover, we would not know how to reproduce, as the result of frequent recourse to the Gospels. At the most, just a few artists who were at the same time contemplatives and saints have managed to convey to us some traits of this mysterious image without deforming or weakening them too much.

So true is this that, for us as for the apostles, faith, far from necessarily dimming our sight or obstructing our view with false representations, can only in reality make our eyes so penetrating that they can reach into the depths of a being and work where they see "things that no eyes has seen and no ear has heard, things beyond the mind of man" (1 Cor 2:9).

However, this is not the place to establish in detail the truth of gospel testimony. That is not my purpose. It is to recall the specific nature of the reality upon which this testimony bears and the involvement of faith demanded for it to be rightly understood. It is, while doing this, to insist upon the irreducible character of Him who "leads us in our faith and brings it to perfection" (Heb 12:2), who gives our faith life, form, and growth.

In former "life of Jesus" undertakings prompted by the scientific positivism then in vogue, the subject of the testimony was not understood or certainly not understood with sufficient depth. Kept at a distance as something interesting or beneficial, it tended to do nothing more than reflect the ideal of the one who "set it up." Bultmann was right in stressing that a real encounter with Jesus postulates an enlistment of subjectivity, an involvement of the whole man in faith. But, "at the limit," this faith has no other object than itself, becoming its own form and content. Does not the "dialogue" with history advocated by Bultmann in the introduction to his *Jesus* then risk ending in solipsism? If faith is not simply the pure identification of the divine action with our own, if it really is *given* and must become operative in us, if it is ordered to that final fulfillment in which

God will be "all in all," it should never fail to be measured against that which provides its ground and nurture.

In Gospel testimony, in actual fact, the mysterious figure of Jesus is proposed to faith as both the wellspring of its rise and the inner law of its growth. He is not an inert object standing before us, whom we could circumscribe by listing Him in one of our categories. Commented on by the whole biblical Word, He embraces a whole universe of meanings. Within them our believing intelligence moves and develops. He leads us ever forward into the depths of the Trinitarian life. At the same time, He resists every attempt at spiritualizing Him, whatever would cause us to lose sight of Him, as if we already possessed the full reality which He makes known to us and to which He leads us. He abides by the reality of our condition as believers, who do not yet live "in vision." At the same time, He continues to supply us with light adapted to our human eyes to illuminate and vivify our faith.

The mysterious figure of the Jesus of the Gospels, without losing the firm traits presented to us in the New Testament, is itself endowed with an internal and an all-pervasive life force which is nothing else but that of the Word of God. We meet them all throughout Scripture in the relation of the Old to the New Testament and in the passage from the one to the other, from promise to fulfillment, from figure to reality. Such is the dynamic and for us incomparable relationship between the Old and the New Testament and also between the historical Jesus and the glorious Christ become a "life-giving Spirit" (1 Cor 15:45).

Harmony in Design: Christmas to Easter

It is interesting to remark that the liturgical year, which scans the full scope of the Church's life of faith and prayer, is organized according to the same structure. It first developed, as we know, around the celebration of the Paschal

Mystery reproduced each Sunday, the Lord's day. But very soon a Christmas-Epiphany cycle took shape which, with the Easter-Pentecost cycle, came to form a kind of second center for the liturgical year, developing together into the figure of an ellipse. The formation of this second center responded to a need of faith, the same in fact, as Ernst Käsemann reminds us, as that which brought about the writing of the Gospels, the setting down of recollections about Jesus.

Besides the Paschal Mystery, Christmas-Epiphany, too, has its own significances; "besides," however, does not mean "independent of." In celebrating the Eucharist, the Pasch of the Lord, the Church continues to keep Christmas. And to celebrate Easter, she begins by calling to mind the abasement of Him who came to us in the extreme weakness of the flesh and goes on to celebrate His triumph over the flesh, mortal as it is, and marked by the dramatic after-effects of sin. These two centers of the mystery of faith, which nourish the prayer of the Church, operate together as a kind of harmonious whole for the realization of a common end.

Historically, their relationship has always been maintained with difficulty. With Bultmann, as we have seen, the Christmas-Epiphany cycle, with its interjection of the earthly and its positive presentation of a mystery that unfolds in time, is absorbed into the Easter cycle, which, as a result, is in danger of losing its roots. But in the Protestant tradition, with which Bultmann's position claims kinship, the accent has sometimes been placed, conversely, on the Christmas-Epiphany cycle, with the risk of robbing the faith of that "consummation" of God's gift with the real regeneration flowing from it. A certain kind of pietism and—more closely linked to it than is apparent—liberalism have both had a tendency in the past or are still so inclined today, to stop short at considering the man Jesus: pietism to be attracted and touched by the crib and the "thorn-crowned head"; liberalism, to be moved to magnify the nobility of soul, the depth of religious experience or even, in the case of some "death of God" theologians, the "contagious" liberty of Him who had to be, but also chose to be, the unique expression and model of the ideal for Christians.

The Catholic world has not always done any better in keeping a perfect balance in the living relationship between the two focuses of Christ's mystery. In the first Christian centuries and perhaps in the East even today, Christians were happiest in contemplating an eminently human Christ who, however, already allowed His divine majesty to shine through His manhood. The Middle Ages, particularly toward their close, took greater delight in Christ's human traits and, in the nineteenth century, the Saint Sulpice school of piety practically failed to go beyond them.

For some time now we have been witnessing a widespread reaction against the "popular piety" that has been called the *devotio moderna* (which seems at present rather a *vetus devotio*) and especially against the sentimentalism of Saint Sulpice. However, in 1938 Father Henri de Lubac, in his first great book, warned of the danger, which he did not consider remote, of a new form of gnosis, drawn out from the doctrine of the Mystical Body and inclined to abandon, or rather to disdain, the modest figure of the Jesus of the Gospels, particularly the Synoptics.[28] In 1954 the review *Christus* initiated its first number by conducting an inquiry which revealed that a great number of Christians questioned liked most to relate to the theological Christ of the Pauline epistles, to Christ "become a life-giving spirit" (1 Cor 15:45), rather than to the historical Jesus presented in the first three Gospels. All these tendencies could represent real deviations if they actually implied the rejection of what, happily, they generally content themselves with leaving in the shade.

Without Easter, in fact, Epiphany remains just some touching human, even if "religious," pages. But without Christmas-Epiphany, Easter loses substance. It would no longer be a victory of God in and over the world. Christianity would tend to be resolved into the advent and triumph of an idea or a line of preaching. It would no longer be the Paschal Mystery revealing the Gospel of us and, with it, the whole New Testament. Is not the substance of Gospel testimony always this: it is the *same Jesus* whom we (or His disciples) have seen, heard, and touched during His mortal life and whom we (or His disciples) have seen, heard, and touched alive again after His death? Without a doubt, His mode of resurrected presence is altogether new, since it has passed through death, which is, in a certain sense, its suppression. Yet He is indeed always *He*.

As has been said, the Gospels were not meant to offer us a simple life of Jesus but to lead us to share faith in Him. By showing us the mystery of His hidden divinity, the Gospels, written as they were in the light of Easter, are fully understood only by Easter faith; but they do not fail to refer us to Christ the man, to the Word of God Incarnate, who came to share our temporal condition. The light of Easter, far from dimming the vision of those who look upon the man Jesus, rather unveils the eyes of believers. The work of paschal faith is not to absorb everything into its brilliance but, on the contrary, to make it possible for us to perceive the whole meaning and to recognize the full worth of the Christmas-Epiphany mystery. Today it seems that, of the two mysteries, the significance of Christmas-Epiphany needs greater stress than Easter's, that it, than the eschatological fulfillment commemorated at Paschaltide. What, in fact, gives the Paschal Mystery its materiality, assures its realism, and prevents its reduction to a Christian ideology is the conviction that it truly "completed" the whole intervention of God in our world, His entire "passage" in the days of the Old Testament, historically realized in the manifestation of the Word of God among us and finally "consummated" on the cross.

The whole mystery encompasses a single coming, expresses the same love in an identical saving gesture, is the fruit of one and the same Spirit. But to restore or to keep the full reality of the gesture made to us, it must be amplified throughout the dimensions of time. We must not take our place within the accomplished reality without passing through the process of accomplishment. To truly understand the "last things" and really make them our own, we should not fail to take into serious consideration the "things-before-the-last." It is well to follow Bonhoeffer's lead by repeatedly reminding ourselves never to separate the three "mounts" of the manifestation and work of Christ—the incarnation, the cross, and the resurrection.

> In Jesus Christ we have faith in the incarnate, crucified and risen God. In the incarnation we learn of the love of God for his creation; in the crucifixion we learn of the judgment of God upon all flesh; and in the resurrection we learn of God's will for a new world. There could be no greater error than to tear these three elements apart; for each of them comprises the whole. Incarnation, cross, and resurrection must be made manifest in their unity and in their difference.[29]

Christmas-Epiphany not only assures the realism of the Paschal Mystery but it is also an annunciation and anticipation of it as well. In some regards, it is already the Paschal Mystery, the mystery of our salvation extended in temporal existence, in this time and in this sensible world which constitutes the place and fabric of our human life. Here is the mystery of the cross and the glory of God, still enveloped in flesh, in human time, in palpable and daily existence. Christmas and the whole hidden life, but also indeed the whole earthly life of Jesus, are already the reality of the cross and the whole paschal reality too, the entire painful and powerful reality of love lived in secrecy, in "mystery," before being completely disclosed and "consummated" in actual death and before the full meaning of all suddenly bursts forth in the light of Easter.

Christmas is not a mystery of suffering reaching its culmination in death; nor is it the mystery of God's glory evident in the full power of His triumph: it is the mystery of suffering and of death and of divine glory already secretly present in everyday existence.

From this point of view, the Christmas mystery and the mysteries of the hidden life following it—about which the Gospels have so little to say—have no less importance, are fraught with no less reality (as Christian piety has generally discerned) than all that has been told us about the public life of Jesus, His teaching and His wonderful works. In fact there we reach, better perhaps than in the discourses or the accounts of Jesus' miracles, the very base of His existence, of His way of being in the world, as we say today, of His mission. There we see Him wholly given up to the will of the Father and at the same time given to men, involved in their history, the story of their sin and servitude, in a way too mysterious for words.

And so the mysteries of Christmas, of Epiphany, and of the hidden life keep us from ever making the revelation of Jesus into a pure "word" in the sense of "mere words" detached from the inexhaustible reality which is its origin and ground. These mysteries preserve the full consistency, the whole truth, of the saving "Yes" of God. They keep before our eyes the grace of a revelation not only prophetic but truly incarnated. In other words, they confirm the truth of the fulfillment sealed on Easter day. And they make it possible, by that very fact, for our paschal faith, for the new life inaugurated in the Holy Spirit, to be realized effectively in the concrete reality of our human existence. The virtue of the Christmas-Epiphany mystery is that it binds our paschal faith to the very flesh of the Lord, by which it must always be nourished.

Christian Life: Hidden and Public

To the infrangible object of our faith represented by the Christmas-Epiphany mystery corresponds a fundamental structure of the spiritual life. The mystery of the Word Incarnate, in a life hidden from the eyes of men, lives again, to a high degree, in the mystery of prayer. Both are a mystery of acceptance, of abnegation, of poverty, of renunciation, of abandonment: a mystery of hiddenness, of a life with value only in the eyes of God and of faith. Both are a mystery of night bringing light, of oblivion and solitude, which is at the same time presence and communion. Both represent, in our world, the existence of a secret that bears the hope and salvation of the world.

Here again, surely, we should not separate this mystery of acceptance and hiddenness from what manifests and consecrates its virtue. The mystery of Easter-Pentecost gives definitive meaning to the Christmas-Epiphany mystery by fulfilling the hope and salvation first brought to us by Christmas-Epiphany. Easter completes the regeneration of that flesh in which, at Christmas, the mystery of the Savior-Word remains hidden. Thus, in prayer, paschal faith and the power of the Spirit of Pentecost prevent contemplation of the Word Incarnate from degenerating into a purely imaginative and sentimental piety, that is, into daydreaming and subtle self-seeking. Just as the power of God, even though buried in our earth but simply just because it is the power of God, "a light that the darkness could not overcome" (Jn 1:5), had to triumph over the darkness bent on imprisoning and overcoming it, so prayer, the superlative sign of faith sunk in the depths of existence, must shine forth in practical charity to renew the face of the earth.

The triumph of God's glory over the darkness of the world can be glimpsed, but only glimpsed, at Epiphany. The disciples too were to catch a fleeting glance at it, but only that, at the time of the Transfiguration and perhaps in connection with some miracle or other. So we, too, in prayer, can get a lightning look at the marvels of love which God has prepared for those who love Him and which He intends to accomplish through their mouths, through their hands, to give witness before the world and in the world to the regenerating power of His resurrection and of the Spirit flowing out of His resurrection to be poured over our whole world.

But just as the triumph of Easter is a triumph of God's power and glory hidden in the depths and powerlessness of flesh; just as the Spirit of love, destined to fill and transform the earth, arises from the fountainhead of Him whose divinity could at first be recognized only by the Father "who sees in secret," so too the power of God can only be poured out over the world through us when we keep ourselves open to the inpouring of the Spirit of God within us by reliving the mystery of Christmas, of the "hidden" life, in the "secret" of prayer. To "operate" in charity, our faith must be nourished by unfailing contemplation of a human face, the "face of Christ," upon which, for the believer, there already shines the glory of God (2 Cor 4:6).

CHAPTER 3

Where Does Hermeneutics Find Support?

AT THE VERY TIME WHEN THE HISTORICAL JESUS WAS TAK-
ing precedence over demythologizing on the theological
scene, demythologizing itself was already broadening out into
the very general hermeneutical question, being, according to
Bultmann, just one form of it. Even today hermeneutics
remains a timely topic. Some have come to see it as *the*
problem, or at least as the one that conditions the solution of all the others.

Hermeneutics can be defined as the theory of interpretation and is classed at the present time as belonging to
basic research in distinction to exegesis, an applied science.

In its most general form hermeneutics belongs to the
domain of philosophy or the human sciences rather than
theology. It is less determined by a particular subject than
by a commitment to get at meaning, that is, the truth, of
every subject. However, it takes on special importance in
the face of the different objects or great works of the faith
to the extent to which they appear with "mysterious"
dimensions and claim to be bearers of absolute truth. The
need for hermeneutical reflection is plainly evident in the

very first place, although not exclusively, in regard to the revelation attested to by the Bible.

The inspiration dominating this research seems often to lead to consequences like demythologizing or certain theses regarding "the historical Jesus." It is in relation to the direction thus taken that I intend to bring up the matter of hermeneutics, claiming in this case even less than in others to cover the question in all its complexity or to encompass all the considerations connected with it.[1]

The Problem Yesterday and Today

Recognized by a number of theologians as particularly urgent at the present time, the hermeneutical problem is in reality an old problem. Considered from the point of view of the faith, it is as old as Christian thought itself, first formulated by reflection on the renewed significance of the Old Testament writings or of the "Law" in which they were generally summarized, beginning with their fulfillment or culmination as wrought by the manifestation and work of Christ. Thereafter, during the whole Patristic period up until halfway through the Middle Ages, all theology, as Father de Lubac has eloquently demonstrated, was absorbed in reflection, in both a theoretical and practical way, on the meaning or meanings of Scripture.[2]

In modern times, nevertheless, the problem has become especially urgent and taken on new forms. At first, its solution seemed to be definitively discovered. During the era of triumphant positivism an immediate solution to the problem seemed at hand in the exact application of scientific methods, as they were progressively perfected and so made more and more suited to encompass the real data. Truth was purely and simply identified with objectivity.

What was not called into question was the value and significance of the scientific method itself. Now, as there has already been occasion to remark in relation to the problem of the historical Jesus and the attempted "lives of Jesus," experience could already have pointed to the problematical character of a method which so often ended—if not always in regard to details, at least in its general outcomes—in representations of scriptural data that differed widely from each other. Does not the objectivity claimed reflect, in fact, certain quite fixed expectations, certain *a priori,* on the part of those who naively professed to be objective? And, beyond the subjective dispositions of the researcher, was there not another type of subjectivity and *a priori* involved in the absolute claim implied in the scientific method itself and in the mode of inquiry defined by it?

Such are the questions raised by Karl Barth as early as 1922, when, on his own, he proposed an entirely new type of interpretation and commentary on the Epistle to the Romans. Like many others, he had felt the distressing poverty of pastors who, before going up into the pulpit to pass on to others the word of Scripture, had been prepared only by historical study, or, if you will, by scientific objectivity. He added that he did not look down upon the contributions of historical research, but that he did think it necessary to put them in their proper place and to challenge their absolute significance and ultimate value. Historical-critical research places us in the presence of "what is given," but that is still not enough to enable us to comprehend and to explain what the documents under consideration are attesting. "Those who hold to the critical-historical method must be more critical" by showing themselves capable of questioning the real meaning, the warranty for truth, to be found in the results that they obtain. Historical criticism is not the court of final appeal.

For Barth, standing above the historical-critical method and acting as its judge is the Word of Revelation, testified to by the biblical writings, which calls into radical questioning our categories, our methods, our judgments. Insofar as we have not reached this reality, insofar as we have not allowed ourselves to be possessed by it, insofar as this "object," by the very power of affirmation dwelling within it, does not in some way impose upon us, and as long as we continue "to establish" everything by our own procedures, we have not yet come to realize what the documents really contain.

Although Barth reacts against the kind of hermeneutics animated by an exclusive concern for "objectivity," he does not approve the type of interpretation that would allow only the heart and soul of the exegete to speak or even to have the most to say. He much prefers that the "object" invest the very activity of the one seeking to know it and to express its full import.

However, the danger of the hermeneutics advocated in his first work and throughout his entire theology of that period lay first in its tie to such a transcendent conception of the Word of Revelation that no bond remained between Word and letter and secondly in the circuitous discourse used to formulate his thought. Later Barth himself recognized that his views at that time made him unable to do full justice to "the humanity of God." In his subsequent work, he set himself to correct this defect.

Bultmann immediately emphasized the excessive independence, not to say unconcern, with which Barth treated the text. He admitted that one could not or should not confine oneself to the analyses made by historical and philological criticism. However, he held that it was necessary to begin with them and to use them to show what the text means.

Bultmann is no less persuaded than Barth of the necessity for the exegete to be involved with his research and to reflect on the place and nature of his involvement. In the preceding chapter, reference has already been made to the idea that he developed of not just "an encounter" but of "a dialogue" with history. In other words, he postulates that the exegete take an altogether different attitude than that of an impartial and indifferent spectator. Throughout his work, he has never left off reiterating the decisive importance of the position taken in regard to these questions. This is why the hermeneutical problem is for him primordial. The interpretation of a text is determined by the way we interrogate it. If we ask nothing of it, if we simply remain passive toward it, a text can say nothing to us. In other words, every interpretation presupposes "a living rapport" between the interpreter and "the thing" which he seeks to discover; it implies a sort of secret alliance with what the text is saying. This living rapport can be of very different kinds, depending on the evident nature of the document itself, whether a mathematical treatise, a work of fiction, a report, or indeed on the special interest and preparation which the interpreter himself brings to it, such as a knowledge of the era or the author. A researcher's interest can enter into his life more or less deeply, and, far from proving an obstacle to his receptivity, normally governs its extent. The more interested he is, the more open he will be.

The living rapport between a researcher and the reality dealt with in the text is, obviously, particularly needed when it is a matter of interpreting the Bible. For what the biblical text conveys is of more interest to the reader than anything else at all. It is not a question of just one truth among others but of the truth that ought to illuminate our whole life and everything in it. Of course, the indispensable living rapport here is basically established by God speaking to me. Just the same, the more deeply I pursue my questioning in regard to God, the more I realize that it produces no answer and that this can only come to me as an entirely free gift through the contingent and always actual meeting with the Word reaching me through the biblical text. I shall never grasp the meaning of the text if I cannot bring an absolute readiness to it. The full mobilization of my whole subjectivity, far from blocking an encounter with the Word of God attested to in Scripture, opens the way for me to reach its living reality.

At a time when the positivism of some of the theologies and exegeses of the last century saw truth as immediately identified with objectivity, the hermeneutics supported by Bultmann tended to align itself completely on the side of subjectivity. Kierkegaard had already written a formula which, if taken in one way, could be repeated by Bultmann, "Truth is subjectivity." But if faith is the appropriation or realization of this truth, is it going to be able to retain an essential reference to a reality other than iself? Is not the absence of a middle term between the divine initiative and the human response going to lead to considering faith as being wholly and indifferently either of God or of man? Or, again, does not "the living rapport" then absorb the very terms which it is supposed to unite? And is not faith going to take on again the form of "an act" without real content, a receiving without a recipient, a "call" without a voice?

Gerhard Ebeling's Theology of the Word

Accepting the best of Bultmann's hermeneutical princi-ples, Gerhard Ebeling has unquestionably extended their scope. He does not consider just the encounter of the exegete with the scriptural text and the resultant necessity for him to span the chasm of twenty centuries during which men have, in a sense, changed the world. He knows that history cannot be defined just in terms of the "historicity" of personal existence, which is only one possible condition among others. His knowledge of history, together with the subtlety of his speculative thought, have led him to direct his interest to "the historicity of the Church and of its preaching," according to the title of one of his early works.[3]

With this in mind, he developed a whole broad theology of the word, a word which, for him, merges with the very thrust of reality. Man awakens to existence by hearing himself called, "Adam, where are you?" and so finds himself at once in a world of the word, a world which, at the same time that it is revealed as question and summons, seems to be waiting for him to respond.

In this universe of the word, the word of God is not accounted with the words of the world. On this point, Ebeling, much more than Bultmann, has recourse for authority to Dietrich Bonhoeffer. Bonhoeffer's influence on him is marked, and Bonhoeffer denounced the ill effects of thinking "in two different compartments." The word of God, Ebeling explains, is not just a higher degree of the sort of talk that goes on between people and is the only kind of communication that they generally designate as speech. The word of God is transmitted by the same organs, realities belonging to our world. Like all speech, it conveys meaning, establishes communication. What sets it apart is that it alone is communication in its fullness and that everything spoken finds its completion, its whole meaning only in and through it. For all speaking is more than a simple transmission of a static content of "ideas." It indicates a meaning, that is, it points to an end, "evokes" a reality which it really makes happen and which it communicates and shares. It is proper to God's word to lead all reality to its end, to give to everything its true and final meaning. It is unparalleled affirmation and accomplishment. It alone expresses and makes it possible to express the truth about man and the whole of reality. It is opposed to the word of men as the word of a truth-teller is opposed to the word of a liar.

Man is, in fact, imprisoned in untruth, in illusion, in darkness. For him the world is truly meaningless; his existence has no future and is given over to vanity and death

as long as he has not heard the saving word which would
deliver him from the law of self-sufficiency, of sin and
death, and open up to him an infinite world of promise.
We can understand the word of God only by beginning with
the Gospel. To express it more accurately, the word of
God is that illuminating and vivifying power that continually actualizes our passage from the Law to the Gospel,
from darkness to light, from death to life. In this cease-
lessly renewed passover man and the universe find meaning
and fulfillment.

Hermeneutics serves this work, this passover. Its objective is for the word to be realized as word. It is something entirely different from a formal undertaking with no
intrinsic relationship to the object to which it is applied.
Rather is it active participation in the very operation of the
word. It becomes a part of the process by which reality
is revealed and attains its end. Contrary to what rigid
orthodoxy always fears, it does not harm God's word to
apply to it evaluative measures which are external to it
and threaten to destroy it. On the contrary, hermeneutics
makes it possible for the word of God to be really understood. Its "content" and "subject" are none other than "the
event of the word as such."

Here we have the reason why critical research and vital
preaching are bound so closely together that they overlap.
Hermeneutics is always developed within a given reality, the
actual significance of which it aims to reveal and even to
realize. In the best sense of the word, it is tradition to the
extent that it brings about the coincidence of the *traditum,*
a reality handed down, with the *actus tradendi,* the very
act by which the reality is transmitted. Here we have a demanding undertaking which postulates honesty in critical
research directed at coming to know *traditum* for what it
is and care to restore its meaning and to understand and

make understood what it has to say. Within the hermeneutical viewpoint, the opposition between historical-
critical theology and practical (or dogmatic) theology tends
to be overcome. They fully support one another, as do
theology and preaching. In fact, says Ebeling, transposing
a saying of Kant, "Theology without preaching is empty,
and preaching without theology is blind."

Hermeneutics has a care for the Church's preaching and
grants its claim to historicity. The concern it shows involves
a spiritual signification. The *locus* to which the word of
God comes and where the real "word of faith" is spoken
is, according to Ebeling, conscience, or more precisely,
conscience in reality, conscience in the world. The conscience at issue here is not the psychological conscience of
idealism, and even less mere moral conscience. It is the
principle of responsible action, the consciousness that brings
with it man's response to the overtures of history and of
tradition, which opens up to him "his field of action." The
heart and very expression of man, conscience is, Ebeling
explains, less "in-stance" than "di-stance," an organ sensi-
tive to the disproportion between what we are and what
we are called to be. It is the place where God's word
never leaves off calling to us and coming to us.

Ebeling's hermeneutics is superior to Bultmann's because
it integrates the inner activity of the living word of revelation as well as the inwardness of "the word of faith" responding to it. The *moment,* that incision into history, is
no longer the one true existent alone in the nudity of its
eruption into reality. The "event of the word" is itself
situated in, inserted into, a process of tradition, a progressive discourse. The future does not become actual in the
present or, to return to the Bultmannian categories, the imperative is identified with the indicative only within the
horizons of an unfinished world, where the field of consciousness remains open. The actual decision of a man

takes place in the framework of a history calling for continuance. However, the movement of the word as restored
by Ebeling seems to need further clarification. It can be
asked whether Ebeling does not view the movement as such
as conveying absolute value. At times, faith seems to merge
purely and simply with the historical venture. To believe
would consist essentially in questioning, that is, in critically
interrogating, the "givens" of tradition. The monuments of
this tradition serve in some way as a springboard to unend-
ing research. The research is not instituted within some
fundamental attachment. It retreats farther and farther
from any such adherence. No attachment, no object constitutes its unifying factor. That function is filled by the
research itself, or, at least, by the negativity that is its soul.

This view fails to give enough value to acknowledging
the "veracity" which, according to Ebeling, characterizes the
Word of God. His Word is essentially affirmation and fulfillment, ideas implied by the untranslatable German word
used by Ebeling— *Zu-sage*. God's Word is basically the
Yes uttered in the promises of a faithful God, a God who
does not deceive, a *Yes* that we will always have to decipher
and translate anew and that must first be heard by an equally faithful listening in the precise place where it was formulated, indissociably united with and contained within
the biblical word and that matchless history culminating in
the body of Jesus Christ, given over to death and brought
back to life again. How truly does it give meaning to
everything and lead everything to its fulfillment. All that it
implies is discerned only if our existence and the whole
world are illumined by it. But this transformation is carried
out only by means of the unique word and on the firm
ground of the first fulfillment of this history. The only true
Christian faith is one which, throughout its entire development, is animated and informed by the unique word and
the unique history which are its foundation.

The Objectivity of the History of Revelation

In Wolfhart Pannenberg we find the beginnings of a hermeneutics with an appreciation not only for real history but also, along with the "historicity" of personal existence, the singular point of emergence at which this history is fulfilled as "proleptic," that is, in its anticipatory and preparatory role: the destiny of Jesus Christ, culminating in His resurrection. Oscar Cullman too claimed to be and made himself the advocate of a hermeneutics shaped by the internal structure of revelation history and, therefore, opposed a hermeneutics proceeding only from a consideration of the "historicity" of existence in general, that which affects every object of human experience. In the works of these two men, whatever reservations and dissatisfactions may be expressed about them in other regards, hermeneutics is not presented as the activity of a subjectivity with a tendency to devour its object or as a movement ready to set itself up as absolute. It recovers the support which makes it possible for it to be presented as a service to a faith fully maintaining its Christian character. This is why, while fully recognizing the unquestionable importance of the hermeneutical problem, these theologians refuse to become immured in it or even to take undue satisfaction in it. For the same reason, it will be enough at this point to indicate the interesting corrective provided by these works to an orientation with the dangers and deficiencies that I have insisted upon pointing out.

Reductive Hermeneutics: Archeology and Teleology

At this point I would like to call attention to another type of hermeneutics which theology recognizes as a radical challenge but to which it has given only a confused response. Yet to theology will perhaps fall the task of verifying the irreplaceable function of the images by which it

lives. Paul Ricoeur characterizes hermeneutics of this kind
as reductive. The theologians whom we have met so far,
in spite of the decided place which they give to criticism
in their hermeneutics, remain characterized by what Ricoeur
calls a care for the recovery or restoration of meaning.
Since the nineteenth century and with renewed emphasis
today, another hermeneutic is coming to the fore. It undertakes to "unmask, to demystify, and to reduce illusion."
Its protagonists are those "masters of suspicion"—Marx,
Nietzsche, and Freud. We will limit ourselves to select-
ing some reflections made by Ricoeur regarding Freud in
his work *De l'interprétation*.[4]

Ricoeur emphasizes the unquestionable contribution made
by reductive hermeneutics. It has been his aim to understand its authoritative voices, which nobody today can allow himself to ignore. At first, it seems nothing but a negation of restorative hermeneutics. According to Ricoeur,
we can reflect more upon it and make full use of it only by
bringing it to interact dialectically with restorative hermeneutics, which at first sight it seems to negate. This
dialectic opens up a new "hermeneutical field," which the
living consciousness ought to keep on exploring with openness.

That the two types of hermeneutics have a common
characteristic becomes immediately apparent.

> Whether one looks back to the will to power of the
> Nietzschean man, to the generic being of the Marxist
> man, to the libido of the Freudian man or whether
> one looks ahead to the transcendent home of significa-
> tion which we designate here by the vague term of
> "sacred," the home of meaning is not consciousness
> but something other than consciousness.[5]

According to this statement, reflection which alone has

the capacity to arbitrate the "hermeneutical conflict" is continually impelled to keep reaching out beyond itself. It is driven to an endless pursuit of the home of meaning, which is ever beyond reach.

It is in relation to the transcendent home of meaning that "Freudian realism" finds its indefeasible value at the same time that it calls for its transcendental justification. How, in fact, can we avoid asking ourselves the question, "What reality? Reality of what?" But of the indefeasible value of this realism Ricoeur says:

> It attests to the nonautonomy of knowledge, its rootedness in existence, the latter being understood as desire and effort. Thereby is discovered not only the unsurpassable nature of life, but the interference of desire with intentionality, upon which desire inflicts an invincible obscurity, an ineluctable partiality. Thereby, finally, is confirmed truth's character of being a task: truth remains an Idea, an infinite Idea, for a being who originates as desire and effort, or, to use Freud's language, as invincibly narcissistic libido.[6]

However, after recognizing the value of psychoanalytic regression, Ricoeur remarks, "In order to have an *arche* (an origin or beginning), a subject must have a *telos* (an end)." He goes on to say:

> The subject, we said above, is never the subject one supposes. But if the subject is to attain its true being, it is not enough for it to discover the inadequacy of its self-awareness, or even to discover the power of desire that posits it in existence. The subject must also discover that the process of "becoming conscious," through which it *appropriates* the meaning of its existence as desire and effort, does not belong to it, but

belongs to the meaning that is formed in it. The subject must mediate self-consciousness through spirit or
mind, that is, through the figures that give a *telos* to
this "becoming conscious." The proposition that there
is no archeology of the subject except in contrast to
a teleology leads to a further proposition: there is no
teleology except through the figures of the mind, that
is to say, through a new decentering, a new dispos-
session, which I call spirit or mind, just as I used the
term "unconscious" to designate the locus of that
other displacement of the origins of meaning back
into my past.[7]

And Ricoeur comes to the conclusion that

the true philosophical basis for understanding the
complementarity of these irreducible and opposed
hermeneutics in relation to the mytho-poetic forma-
tions of culture is the dialectic of archeology and
teleology.[8]

We could be led to believe that here is a fertile ground
for theology, where original work is to be done within a
certain "culture" or, if you will, a particular tradition.
Theology, in fact, puts us in the presence of a certain number of "figures" that are proposed to us as possessing a
meaning destined to be realized within us. The appropriation of this meaning also postulates a real decentering of
consciousness, just as accession to the faith always passes
through a renunciation of the inauthentic self of sinning
man.
    According to Ricoeur, the *symbol* is where the dialectic
between archeology and theology, and between regression
and progression, takes place; and the symbol has to be interpreted in accordance with the same dialectic. In its

varied forms, the symbol is, in fact, characterized by a structure of double or multiple meanings.

> A symbol exists, I shall say, where linguistic expression lends itself by its double or multiple meanings to a work of interpretation. What gives rise to this work is an intentional structure which consists not in the relation of meaning to thing but in an architecture of meaning, in a relation of meaning to meaning, of second meaning to first meaning, regardless of whether that relation be one of analogy or not, or whether the first meaning disguises or reveals the second meaning. This texture is what makes interpretation possible, although the texture itself is made evident only through the actual movement of interpretation.[9]

Toward the end of his work, Ricoeur returns to the reflections on the symbol with which he opened it, situating them within the perspectives of the two types of hermeneutic which he has illustrated.

> Pursuing this analysis of the intentional structure of symbols more deeply, I would say that the opposition between regression and progression, which we have struggled to establish and to overcome at the same time, throws light on the paradoxical texture described as the unity of concealing and showing. True symbols are at the crossroads of the two functions which we have by turns opposed to and grounded on one another. Such symbols both disguise and reveal. While they conceal the aims of our instincts, they disclose the process of self-consciousness.[10]

In this way the symbol defines a horizon which appears as the background as well as the foreground of the living, interpretive intelligence. Working within the symbol, the intelligence itself unfolds while contributing to the formation of the symbol.

When faced with symbols, hermeneutical research could be in danger of coming to a halt. Then symbols would lose their revelatory virtue. Hermeneutics has inalienable importance and signification for the life of faith as well as, more generally, for encountering a reality always to be sought beyond the things that reveal it. The necessary work of interpretation that it does should not, for its part, claim to diminish the world of symbols within which it is carried on.

Truth in a Faithful and Creative Telling

The sum total of reflections devoted to the hermeneutical problem leads to the conviction, which is becoming more general, that an illusion is implied in the scientific ideal of pure objectivity. Hermeneutical reflection has brought to light the necessity for taking into consideration, or rather for actively mobilizing, the subject in the disclosure and appropriation of every reality. Such taking into consideration, such mobilization, is even more imperative when there is a question of reality which *speaks* because it is permeated with thought and life. Hermeneutical care originates in the correct conviction that in the realm of faith, as in every other domain, man reaches truth at the end of a search.

However, the part played by the subject is sometimes given such emphasis that truth seems less the foundation and objective of the activities of the human mind than their product. Or the idea that truth must be sought becomes so impressive that the search for truth is apt to be taken for truth itself. In both cases, whatever the description given to its functioning, conscious subjectivity fills the whole field of reality. The "meaning" of existence and with it of all reality is totally given in the lightning flash of an encounter or in the trajectory of a never-ending question. It has no constituent preexistence in the conscious subject.

One advantage of Freudian analysis is to show that "the subject is never what one believes," and that it becomes what it is less by its own doing than by the mediation of the structured reality to which it belongs as a component. From another perspective, Hegel could criticize the illusions of an unmediated subjectivity, unaware that it can only be realized within a milieu of "figures" through which it must pass and by which "meaning" is disclosed to it in the very process of becoming itself.

Certainly faith has no obligation to subscribe to all these systems; but, as long as it resists the temptation to idealism, it will be apt to consider itself within perspectives that conform to those structures of reality brought to light by these views. Faith emerges and flowers within the alternating play of light and darkness, of presence and absence. In its rise, as all throughout its intellectual and practical becoming, faith is animated by what Ricoeur calls a "transcendent home of signification." It always remains veiled within the mystery which is its foundation and true nourishment, but which becomes present in consciousness only through the historical "figures" that reveal it.

Moreover, a hermeneutics conformed to its functional nature, that does not take itself for its own principle and end, that is not the expression of faith, but rather finds in faith a place for its questions and a support for its movement, must always remain ordered to the exploration of these figures, with respect for their internal structure and participation in their movement. For these figures of revelation are themselves engaged in a life-giving discourse that finds its meaning converging and concentrated in the peerless and unfathomable figure of Jesus Christ. In relation to theology, hermeneutics must contribute to the constant

effort needed to recover the thread of this discourse. The
truth that it then helps to uncover and, in this sense, comes
to serve as an instrument is not constituted by it. If hermeneutics can lay claim to serving faith, its purpose must
be, above all, to establish rules for discourse or, if you will,
for faithful "translation."

CHAPTER 4

Is the World
Moving toward
Complete Secularization?

THE PROBLEMS OF DEMYTHOLOGIZING, OF THE HISTORICAL
Jesus, and of hermeneutics have chiefly concerned contemporary man's encounter with biblical testimony and
have been, for the most part, the special province of
German-speaking theologians. For some years now, these
problems have tended to fade into the background in the
face of a more general problem which includes them as
well: secularization. This time the thrust comes not so
much from beyond the Rhine as from across the English
Channel and, beyond that, the Atlantic Ocean. As a matter
of fact, it bids fair to spread over all Christian countries.
And as it no longer has anything immediately to do with
deciphering documents, a task demanding techniques of
analysis and more or less scholarly study, but arises from
the consciousness of a situation affecting the whole world,
we see it reaching and being discussed in spheres far outside of specialized theology. Its interest, as well as its complexity, stems from the fact that it concerns not just a single
aspect of Christian faith but its whole significance. It is

for this reason that the question of Christian identity stands
out more sharply and urgently in this context than in any
other.[1]

The Actual Situation

The phenomenon of secularization can be defined as the
constantly increasing tendency for the realities of human
life and of the world to establish their own autonomy apart
from the whole sacred, religious, and ecclesial order. Its
factual existence can hardly be disputed. It is found in
practically every sector of life and is progressively reaching all over the world, even if it is not everywhere maintained with the same assurance.

In the social sphere, many services which depended for
a long time on private initiative and were generally associated in Christian countries with church-related institutions, have been taken over by civil, "secular" society—hos-
pitals, "homes," schools. . . . In the political sphere, a long
time has passed since the clergy constituted a social "order"
as they did in France during *l'Ancien Régime*. In cases
where "Christian" parties have not yet been brought to an
end, their very existence is frequently challenged. Public
opinion, Christian as well as non-Christian, is less and less
willing to allow the Church as such to intervene in electoral
campaigns or political debates with moral repercussions
(laws about divorce and contraception, for example). In
the cultural and artistic realm, religious themes and forms
can, of course, be presented—except in certain dictator-
ships—but not in their own right and on their own authority. They can appear, along with other productions, on
radio and television programs, for example, by becoming
part of a general non-religious framework.

As to theology, which normally treats of the sacred order
of revelation and so has reference to some confessional institutions, in a number of countries it long ago became suspect

and even excluded by the officially promoted culture. And in the world as a whole its status is increasingly challenged and its place diminished. At times, it is true, it has been reintroduced into university teaching by being smuggled in by the roundabout routes of history, literature, or philosophy—in other words, by secularizing it. If, in our culture, preeminence is accorded any discipline, it is not given to theology, as would have been the case in the religious world of the Middle Ages, but to science. Not only is science definitively emancipated from any religious tutelage; rather it seeks to impose its own laws, considered as indefeasible, on religious objects themselves, and on the Bible first of all.

The beginning of this process far antedates our times. Without overemphasizing the importance of its origin, Dietrich Bonhoeffer, who made it a favorite theme for reflection at the end of his life and under whose patronage much research continues to be carried on, traced its beginning to the thirteenth century, that is, to the era when Christianity, having attained its apogee, began to show the first signs of breaking down. The French Revolution, joined with the Enlightenment movement, clearly marked an important stage in the process. The revolution of 1789 was, in a way, a triumphant affirmation of reason and liberty in the political and social spheres. It set itself in direct opposition to the order and tradition inherited from the past, which until then had been viewed as a reflection of an intangible, sacred, and hierarchically constituted nature.

Bonhoeffer thought that this great movement had reached its culmination in our era. This judgment, which he formulated in another way by stating that the contemporary world had come of age, could doubtless be disputed and distinctions made about it. However, even if it is true that men and institutions today remain for the most part prisoners of obscure taboos or new and enslaving idols, the secularization of human life and thought has arisen from a certain number of undeniable realities which no one seriously wishes to contest. The autonomy of science is, in principle, generally admitted, but we ought to bear in mind that the scientific point of view is not the only point of view. It is a fact too that in all religious denominations, biblical criticism is increasingly accepted and carried on without hesitation. Also, democratic pluralism is quite generally considered the normal form of contemporary society, except for states called totalitarian precisely because they do not conform to the norm. All this amounts to admitting that, at least in certain aspects, religious things and institutions can or ought to resemble profane things and institutions.

If, as an experienced fact, the progress of secularization, like the development of socialization, cannot be denied, judgments about it can vary from individual to individual and from one school of thought to another. Some have come to see it as a calamity that has overtaken Christianity or as a specter that must be warded off. For them secularization simply means the diminishment of the world of faith. Others, on the contrary, see it as something good, or at least as a new opportunity offered to Christianity, if not a direct means of realizing its deepest meaning. The Church has not authorized in any conciliar statement such an immediate, and certainly optimistic, identification of world progress with the realization of Christian truth. Nevertheless, she is far from turning a cold shoulder to all the projects which the world is attempting to carry out. Rather, she sets herself to discern the "signs of the times" so that she may recognize God's invitation in them.

She sees herself as called upon to take a servant's place in a world on the march, to renounce every domineering attitude, every seeking for human privilege, every yielding to a ghetto spirit of any kind. It certainly has not been her wish to bless or encourage every form of secularization but still less has it been her desire to anathematize it.

Actually, as with other things in life, secularization is ambiguous. It is a question put to us Christians or, if you will, a trial, in the positive sense of the word, of our faith, that is, an occasion for all that is true in our faith to be strengthened. For that to be accomplished we stand in imperative need of clarity of mind and vigilance of spirit.

Our obligation to do this becomes quite clear when we come up against some strange analogies between positions at first apparently opposed to one another. Could not one example be the striking analogy between the more or less traditionalist program of establishing the social reign of Jesus Christ and what Bonhoeffer formulated in stating that Christ should not be just "an object of religion" but ought to become in fact what He really is—the Lord of the world?

Following his experience in the United States, Bonhoeffer also remarked that the complete separation of Church and State is not necessarily the best means of realizing the spiritual vocation of the former and the real independence of the latter. This simplistic solution, he explains, tends to create rivalry between the two, since they are inclined to work on the same plane. For example, while the Church is going ahead with developing more or less closed educational and cultural systems that are no longer what they ought to be, a leaven for the life of the world, the State will not be better fitted to integrate these elements of the national life under its control. Likewise, when religious congregations do not receive official recognition but continue to exist and of necessity operate outside the law, they could, in extreme cases, pervert the normal context. We know that the first experiment of the priest-workers was judged in different ways by lay Christians. Certainly, it could be taken as an effort at renunciation by the Church in order to share without limits, through some of its official representatives, in the life, trials, and struggles of the world. But to many militant Christians the priest-workers meant an implicit admission that the Church was not really in them present and acting in the world. People are also continually questioning the appropriateness of the Church's taking official positions on political, economic, and social matters, even in defense of the poor and the oppressed. Some have found it possible to ask whether the participation of priests and bishops in strikers' demonstrations might not betray, contrary to the highest intentions of those concerned, a sort of neo-clericalism, somewhat in the same way that neo-colonialism has often taken over from a form of crude colonialism that had become intolerable.

It is important, therefore, to be wary of simplistic unilateral solutions considered as reached once and for all. To close in upon a problem more expeditiously before determining the direction that should be taken and the conditions that should be met to arrive at an acceptable solution, one ought to recall the principal reflections that some theologians have developed on the subject.

Friedrich Gogarten

Friedrich Gogarten (1887-1967) was the first theologian to make secularization the direct theme of his investigation and speculation. In a book published in 1953 entitled *Verhängnis und Hoffnung der Neuzeit: Die Säkularisierung als theologisches Problem,* he wrote:

> At any rate it is clear that the test which secularization represents for the Christian faith and which the latter has to meet for its own sake, increases in urgency and difficulty in the face of a secularized and historicized Christianity. In other words, it now becomes necessary to pose the problem of the Christian faith in a completely new way in the light of secularized

and historicized human existence.[2]

According to Gogarten, secularization began and is deeply rooted historically in biblical faith. What we are experiencing today is only the final issue of a movement which originated in Judeo-Christian revelation. First, through the doctrine of creation, man knows himself as situated "between God and the world," according to the title of another work by the same author; and the world is clearly exorcised of all the dark powers which paganism has always been tempted to see in it. It is above all in Jesus Christ that man is made a son, an heir, of the creator God. God has, therefore, charged him with the task of making all of creation a place for his dominion.[3] Thus St. Paul understands Christians to be freed from every taboo whatsoever. "For me there are no forbidden things," he declares (1 Cor 6:12). It is true that the Apostle adds, "maybe, but not everything does good." Man must therefore perform a work of discernment. He is not to unburden himself of it by putting it on someone else's shoulders or leaving it up to some law or other. Reason is given him to fulfill the task: it is an instrument precisely suited for ruling over the world. He has no right to renounce its exercise; to do so would be to fail in his vocation as a man. It would be to abdicate the responsibility which God Himself has confided to him.

In science, reason is exercised in an eminent way. When complemented by technology, science rescues the world from the hidden forces that have terrorized it, in order to hand it over to the power of man and so to maintain it in its true reality as a world according to God's own design. Faith has the elementary duty of recognizing the autonomy of science and of the human reason that advances it without wanting to dictate to them in any way or even to intervene in whatever may be their exercise. On the other hand, science must remain within its own secular sphere. Its task is to master, bit by bit, the data of experience. It cannot fail, it is true, to try to integrate the various results of these analyses within a total vision that becomes more and more "comprehensive" of the reality made available by its investigations. So the question of totality appears on the horizon more or less of necessity. But, while perhaps asking that question with a rigor that never stops increasing, science can do no more than raise the question, if at least it consents to remain in its own order and not to betray its own nature. In regard to some final and integral meaning, science can do no more than act the part of "an unlearned questioner." Here is why its research, on its own level, never comes to an end and never should.

Nevertheless, it would be a mistake to think that the role of faith is to bring relief to the "unlearned questioner" of science by offering to complete its incompleteness. Rather does faith serve to remind science of the radical openness that acts as its driving power and calls it back to its secular nature. Otherwise, it could, in its own turn, degenerate into "Christian ideology," that is, basically, into "Christian secularism."

Gogarten, who seeks to appreciate fully the value of the phenomenon of secularization, remains, in fact, conscious of its constitutive ambiguity and intends to maintain a critical attitude toward it. For him, faith is the principle of enduring criticism. For faith to act in the capacity it must not, when challenged by secularization, pervert itself. It can, as a matter of fact, be tempted to become withdrawn by taking refuge, for example, in the domain of stark individual ethics or unalloyed absorption in personal salvation. This is the temptation of Hegel's "beautiful soul."

But, on its side, secularization, when cut off from its true principle—the radical distinction between God and the world—carries within itself the seeds of its own perversion.

When man no longer understands himself as a creature of God, he is almost necessarily caught up in "a titanic effort without respite or end," which crushes him by turning him into nothing but an instrument or slave of the ends proposed by his own ideologies. Or, becoming convinced of the emptiness of his enterprises, he may sink into nihilism. A secularization that takes itself for its own principle and end reaches one of two fatal terms, either an inhuman ideology quickly assuming a totalitarian form or a desperate and anarchistic nihilism. History furnishes us with more than one example of this perversion of secularization, which Gogarten calls "secularism." It is nothing else but a substitute for religion. The term will often be repeated, with the same pejorative sense, in the most optimistic analyses of the phenomenon of secularization.

However, while Gogarten allows us to see beyond every naive evaluation, whether optimistic or pessimistic, of secularization, by stressing the indefeasible function that faith must fill, he does little to show us under what conditions this function can continue to be exercised effectively. Is the "wholly other" God to whom he is content to return different enough from the God of Aristotle, so transcendent that the world can follow its course without being affected by Him in any way? On the other hand, is it possible to be content with an absolute cleavage between science and faith, if faith itself, in order not to be its own principle and end, must be able to recognize in the world itself testimony of the one holy God? If it is possible to accept without difficulty Gogarten's point of view insofar as it refers to the order of knowledge where only pure nature is implicated (representing, as it always does, a limit or an abstraction and having only operational, provisional value), the question is less simple when faced with sciences that involve a relationship to the concrete reality to which man belongs and within which, Christianity tells us, God has spoken to us and continues to communicate Himself to us. And this statement is enough to suggest that the idea of radical secularization, even if and when dissociated from the criticism of "secularism," is perhaps not so easily reconcilable, whatever Gogarten may think, with a faith that rests on a revelation accomplished in real history, manifested in the flesh, and reuniting man with the very heart of his existence.

Harvey Cox

Many of Gogarten's ideas have been taken up and brilliantly exploited by Harvey Cox in his famous work *The Secular City*. For him too the roots of secularization are to be found in biblical revelation. "Thus the *disenchantment of nature* begins with the Creation; the *desacralization of politics* with the Exodus; and the *deconsecration of values* with the Sinai covenant, especially with the prohibition of idols."[4] Cox too insists on the necessary distinction between secularization and secularism understood as "an ideology, a new closed world-view which functions very much like a new religion."[5]

The basic thesis of the young Harvard professor is that the secular city is plainly not to be identified with the Kingdom of God but that it does open up new possibilities for Christian faith. With its help, new aspects of the Gospel can be perceived, and it is probably better suited than any other form of civilization to respond to the divine plan, furnished in rough draft and presented in its first realization by the Bible.

In a much more concrete way than Gogarten, Cox sets himself to trace the hopes and tasks given to Christian faith by the birth of the secular city, which we have seen take place. He institutes a sociological analysis of the city, which is being increasingly actualized in the form of "a technopolis," and he does so in the conviction that a theology which would develop without any ties to the realities that are being analyzed by the social, economic, and political sciences and that constitute men's lives in the concrete would condemn itself to sterility and slow death.

The new type of civilization expressed in the modern technopolis is characterized, according to Cox, by two principal traits, anonymity and mobility. People who turn nostalgically to the past usually denounce these two attributes as dehumanizing and as closing the door to the profound experiences characteristic of religion. Nevertheless, Cox asks, does not anonymity preserve privacy, without which there is no true human life? And isn't it the same with mobility—like anonymity, it admits of some dangers but it also frees us from the bonds of servitude. What is more, modern mobility, in the light of the Bible, takes on a more positive meaning. The whole Hebrew vision of God is defined within the social context of a nomadic, an essentially homeless, people.[6] Yahweh is opposed to the Baalim, that is, to the "resident," immobile gods. Not only does he send his people journeying but He goes before them. Likewise, "motifs of mobility and homelessness, of wandering and of pilgrimages informed the self-understanding of the earliest Christian community."[7] The first Christians knew that here they had "no abiding city." One of the oldest titles used to designate them was "a pilgrim people." The Bible, continues the same author, does not call upon man to renounce mobility but orders him to go "to the place that I will show you." "Perhaps the mobile man can even hear with less static a Message about a Man who was born during a journey, spent his first years in exile, was expelled from his own home town, and declared that he had no place to lay his head."[8]

Cox likewise shows the positive significance which, in the light of the Bible, can be recognized in the "style" of secular civilization, characterized as it is by pragmatism

and a sense of the profane. For the pragmatist of the modern city, "Life . . . is a set of problems, not an unfathomable mystery."[9] Could not the conduct of the pragmatist
correspond to a sort of discipline, a kind of modern asceticism? A relationship between the biblical and pragmatic"
concept of truth is easy to see. In the Bible a "true" vine
is one which bears fruit. Jesus says that he *is* the truth
and that his followers should *do* the truth. Not that modern
pragmatism represents an absolute value, stripped of all
ambiguity. We must keep on being vigilant in this matter
so that "pragmatism as a style and a method should never
be allowed to degenerate into pragmatism as a new ontology."[10] Should it do so, we would have "a new closed world-
view" that would write off as useless artistic beauty, poetry
and unproductive beings. To put it more precisely, danger
lies "rather in the catastrophic *narrowing* of the idea of use-
fulness and thus of worth to the purposes and programs one's
own group considers important."[11] Cox likes to see John
Kennedy as an example of a pragmatic style giving expression
to a wholesome secularization. "But in the way he fulfilled
the office, in his quiet refusal to function as the high priest of
the American religion, Kennedy made an indispensable contribution to the authentic and healthy secularization of our
society. He was a supremely political leader."[12]

As for the "profanity" in some way requisite for a
pluralist city, it allows the faith to become disengaged from
its ideological compromises. According to Cox, it is the
blurring of the God of the Bible by the ideas of Plato and
Aristotle that led Camus to think that he had to choose
between God and freedom, between Christian faith and
human creativity. Not that, as some today would be ready
to maintain, there are no real differences between those
who believe in God and those who do not. "But it is precisely to uncover and clarify these real differences that we
must expose and discard the unreal ones."[13] And secu-

larization definitely makes a contribution to this work of clarification. Besides, we do not have the right to interpret the "celebration" of the secular city to which Harvey Cox addresses himself as an exaltation of a world emptied of every manifestation of faith. He even dwells on an analysis of what the proper ministry of the Church could be. Inspired by the Dutch Reform theologian Johannes C. Hoekendijk, he envisages a fourfold ministry.[14] First, a ministry of *kerygma*. "Employing political terminology, the church broadcasts the fact that a revolution is under way and that the pivotal battle has already taken place . . . that the One who frees slaves and summons men to maturity is still in business." Then a ministry of *diakonia,* a ministry "of healing and reconciling, binding up wounds and bridging chasms, restoring health to the organism" like the Good Samaritan. A ministry of *koinonia* consisting in the formation of a truly human city, "a kind of living picture of the character and composition of the true city of man for which the church strives." And finally, a ministry of exorcism, ordered to the denunciation and termination of all idolatries and the liberation of men from what Freud called the "archaic heritage" poisoning the lives of societies as well as of individuals, as the racial problem in the United States eloquently demonstrates.[15]

In another work, Cox, when referring to three of the principal books of the Bible—Exodus, the Psalms and the Apocalypse—lays down the qualities of a Christian community with a constitution to be found in scriptural revelation.[16] It would be a community always open to the future, constantly moving ahead, a community singing its joy and its thanksgiving for the marvelous work to which God Himself calls it; finally it would be a community of people with vision, offering the human venture some dimensions generally unnoticed or neglected and, eventually, it would lead others to adopt these as their own. The fact remains that so far Cox has been much more expansive about the boons of secularization than about its risks and the conditions required for it to remain conformed to its true nature. If it is true that secularization is not the negation of faith, since it is said to stem from it, it is hard to see how faith can continue to regulate secularization without becoming, in its own turn, regulated by it—unless faith keeps constantly referring back to its own true meaning.

Cox distrusts reflection that flows too readily from experience and action, and he is right. But is he not, however, too quick to clip the wings of thought? The extreme reserve that he recommends exercising on the "metaphysical" —or simply the speculative and cognitive—plane can express, as he wants it to do, a sound and needed asceticism, on condition that it is not simply weakness or resignation. He has come to recognize this to some extent during the course of a long debate provoked by his book.[17] Can people, as a matter of fact, be content with taking pragmatic, limited, provisional stands when the technological power of men leads to the construction of arms that make the very existence of humanity questionable? And what of the apparently useless suffering and death that goes on in the secular city and is there as elsewhere the common lot of man, today as yesterday and surely tomorrow as well? In the face of these realities, can we excuse ourselves from asking "final" and, at least in that sense, "metaphysical" questions?

Cox tells us that we ought to be on guard against allowing pragmatism as a style and method to degenerate into a new ontology.[18] But would it not be appropriate to examine more closely just what it is that can keep us vigilant and just what it is that gives grounds for refusing to fall back on the immediately utilitarian? Plato's thought, like Cox's, was meant to be eminently political. It is expressed at its height in the *Republic* and the *Laws*. But Plato was convinced that there is no serious political thought without metaphysics, or where the Good, the True, and the Beautiful are not sought.

Cox certainly distrusts Greek philosophy. To his mind, it has for all too long a time obscured the biblical message. It does, in fact, entail some risks, at least insofar as it has not been shaken up by the disconcerting Word of the living God. But does Cox himself entirely escape from its ill effects, considering that the theology which he proposes, no matter what his intentions are, does reflect a certain dualism between the profane and the only Holy? And is not God's transcendence conceived in such an abstract way that it leaves us afraid that men, and the Church herself, are abandoned to an all too human destiny?

In fact, could the Church hold on to the possibility of being reunited to the source of her kerygma, of her diaconal activity, of her power of exorcism, would she still be able to find the binding strength of that *koinonia* which has to be the sign and leaven of the true city, if she were deprived of all interiority, entirely given over to the external work of building up the earthly city, if the strong chains attaching her to the unique event of her foundation were broken, and if she no longer sought God save in an indeterminate future hereafter? In order for the Church to exercise her ministry, as Cox sees it, she must show that structurally she is infinitely supple, flexible. She must live in tents, not in temples, " a people whose life is informed by its confident expectation that God is bringing in a new regime and that they are already allowed to taste its fruits." She must mold herself as far as possible on the infinitely mobile form of the human community. "We are moving into a stage in which we will need a widely differentiated range of types of church organization to engage a society which is becoming differentiated at an accelerated rate."[19]

The result will be that "the problem of 'church unity,'

the issue which created such widespread interest among religious people in recent years, will not be a matter of divisions between denominations but of the relationship between highly differentiated expressions of the same church."[20]

Who would not admit that there are a number of truths and helpful suggestions in these observations? Nevertheless, it can be asked whether, in the end, this church will still do anything but reflect the motley and broken figure of human society, if it does not run the risk of being reduced to a mere hope without well defined foundations (which according to the faith are established "once and for all") and if, consequently, it will still be able to intervene in the world to some extent and to pronounce over it an authoritative and saving judgment.

Karl Barth

Secularization viewed in the light of biblical revelation as an opportunity given to Christianity has found support in the thought of Karl Barth, who has left his impress upon all contemporary theology. He also offers this line of thought a valuable corrective and a new factor to give it balance.

Barth was, in fact, the first to develop what today has become a commonplace, the opposition between faith and "religion." When he began, his theology was designed, as we know, as a reaction against the liberal theology that had long dominated Protestantism and tended to place Christian faith within a general framework of "religious experience." For Barth, on the contrary, or rather for the Barth of the 1920's, religion, together with all that expresses it on the human level, can only speak the rash pretensions of man's sinful being. Insofar as it develops as a human "possibility," religion does not escape, any more than any other reality, the judgment of the unique Word of God.

In his first great work, a commentary on the Epistle to the Romans,[21] he applies to religion what St. Paul says about the Law in the seventh chapter of his letter. Religion is the expression of the last human possibility.[22] But this possibility is radically limited and does not allow us to encounter a God who is Lord of all reality and could not by that very fact become the term of any human project no matter how great. As a scheme to reach out to touch God, it even evidences the sin that dwells in the heart of man. Seen in this light, religion, like the Law, will be able to find meaning in the order of salvation, since where sin has abounded, God makes grace superabound. But this significance appears only with the coming of the Gospel, which marks the end of sin as well as of the Law.

Later, in his *Church Dogmatics,* Barth was to take up again his reflections on the relationship between religion and revelation and develop them at greater depth, especially by bringing out the nuances of his thought. He knows, he says, that God's revelation can be understood as a human religion and, by that very fact, as one religion among others; but "the point at issue cannot be whether God's revelation has also to be regarded as man's religion and therefore as a religion among other religions. We saw that to deny this statement would be to deny the human aspect of revelation and this would be to deny revelation as such."[23] "But," continues Barth,

> looked at in this way, religion is unbelief. From the standpoint of revelation, religion is clearly seen to be a human attempt to anticipate what God in His revelation wills to do and does do. It is the attempted replacement of the divine work by a human manufacturer. The divine reality offered and manifested to us is replaced by a concept of God arbitrarily and willfully evolved by man.[24]

In Jesus Christ, however, religion, like the whole reality of sinful man, is at once judged, condemned, and saved. Because this is so, Christianity can be spoken of as "the true religion," but only to the extent to which we speak of a justified sinner. Christianity is the true religion to the degree, and only to the degree, that it lives wholly by the grace of God.

> We must insist, therefore, that at the beginning of a knowledge of the truth of the Christian religion, there stands the recognition that this religion too, stands under judgment that religion is unbelief, and that it is not acquitted by any inward worthiness, but only by the grace of God, proclaimed and effectual in his revelation. But concretely, this judgment affects the whole practice of our faith: our Christian conception of God and the things of God, our Christian theology, our Christian worship, our forms of Christian fellowship and order, our Christian morals, poetry and art, our attempts to give individual and social form to the Christian life, our Christian strategy and tactics in the interest of our Christian cause, in short our Christianity, to the extent that it is *our* Christianity, the human work we undertake and adjust to all kinds of near and remote aims and which as such is seen to be on the same level as the human work in other religions. This judgment means that all this Christianity of ours, and all the details of it, are not what they ought to be and pretend to be, a work of faith, and therefore of obedience to the divine revelation.[25]

Even while stressing the distance separating the Word of revelation from all human activities and institutions, including those that are religious, Barth nevertheless recognizes a certain immanence of the light of revelation in our world, and by that very fact, in the historical manifestation of

Christian faith and religion. He explains this other aspect by comparing it to the way the sun shines on the world.

> We have compared the name of Jesus Christ with the sun in its relation to the earth. . . . Without ceasing to be the light of the sun, it becomes the light of the earth. . . . It is the same with the name of Jesus Christ in relation to the Christian religion. The name alone is its justification. But it cannot be transcendent without being immanent. For it is only the Christian religion which is justified by it and that means that it is differentiated and marked off and stamped and characterized by it in a way peculiar to itself. In the light of its justification and creation and election by the name of Jesus Christ, the fact that it is the Christian religion and not another cannot possibly be neutral or without significance. On the contrary, even though Christianity is a religion like others, it is significant and eloquent, a sign, a proclamation. There is an event on God's side—which is the side of the Incarnate Word of God—God adopting man and giving Himself to him. And corresponding to it there is a very definite event on man's side. The event is determined by the Word of God. It has its being and form in the world of religion. But it is different from everything else in this sphere having this form. The correspondence of the two events is the relationship between the name Jesus Christ and the Christian religion from the standpoint of its sanctification. It is not by laws and forces of human religion and therefore of man, but in virtue of the divine foundation and institution, that this particular being and form are an event in the world of human religion.[26]

The Christian religion, being justified by the name of Jesus Christ, from whom it receives its name, is also sanctified by it and becomes a holy reality.

> The Christian religion is the sacramental area created
> by the Holy Spirit, in which the God whose word be-
> came flesh continues to speak through the signs of His
> revelation. And it is also the existence of men created
> by the same Holy Spirit who hear this God continual-
> ly speaking in His revelation. The Church and the
> children of God do actually exist. The actuality of
> their existence is quite unassuming, but it is always
> visible and in its visibility it is significant. It is an
> actuality which is called and dedicated to the declara-
> tion of the name of Jesus Christ. And this is the
> sanctification of the Christian religion.[27]

Barth first seems to burn up everything encompassed by
religion in the fire of God's sanctity and thus to abandon
the whole human reality to its miserable secular self-sufficiency. Then, by virtue of the dialectic between sin and
grace, he retrieves and gives value to all the fundamental
elements postulated for the building up of an authentic
religion. It is to have sacramental reality, visibly "signified"
revelation, taking form in a historical community of faith.
In this way, he marks off the limits that Christianity will
have to impose on the movement of secularization.

Lesslie Newbigin

Barth has not allowed himself to be drawn into more
recent discussions on the future of Christianity in a secularized world. One of the soundest reactions that can be heard
in reply to simplistic or fallacious statements on the matter
is what Bishop Lesslie Newbigin has to say in his book
Honest Religion for Secular Man.[28]

Newbigin has no intention of adopting a position completely opposed to those who take a favorable view of

secularization. But he insists, more than others do, on the conditions needed to defend the secular city—which, in certain aspects, already exists as an inescapable fact—against the ever-present danger of falling into what Cox and Gogarten call secularism. Like them, Newbigin readily recognizes in secularization a movement which does not lack rapport with biblical revelation and the affirmation of the *Tu Solus Sanctus.* But, he first emphasizes, the critical, liberating, exorcising power of faith can only be exercised from the basis of positive certitude and perduring acknowledgment of the Word, of the authority and action of the living God.

> Man cannot live by negation alone any more than he can know by doubt alone. The negation will become self-destructive if it does not rest upon an affirmation which is, for the moment, not questioned. The inexhaustible power of the prophetic spirit in the tradition of biblical faith was derived from a tremendous affirmation—namely, the affirmation of the reality and power and holiness of God . . .[29]

Secularization has certainly acted as an agent of liberty. It can make a notable contribution by rescuing some mission countries from the heavy weight of ancestral servitudes that obstruct evangelization. But in order not to act as a destructive anarchism, liberty must indeed recognize a principle for making choices. As Newbigin puts it, "Eventually the question will have to be faced: what is the authority for the decision which individuals are required to make? As a Christian I answer that the authority is the will and nature of God revealed in Jesus Christ."[30] A principle of judgment provided by faith makes it possible for us to escape from the ambiguity represented by secularism and to ward off the dangers of totalitarianism and nihilism:

It is only in the presence of Christ, the incarnate,
crucified and risen Lord, that we can speak truly
about the world or be truly involved in it. In and
through Christ alone do we know the world as it truly
is, created in God's love, alienated from God's love,
redeemed and renewed by God's love. True Christian
involvement in the world is a life lived in the world
in responsibility to him who is its Lord, and this responsibility means responding to him who has first
acted, answering him who has first spoken, loving him
who has first loved. It is responsibility *to him* who
alone is worthy of our total self-giving. Without this
supernatural reference, the programme of "involvement" can only become that conformity to the world
which is death.[31]

But where are we to find this God who is the guarantor
for our liberty and for the generous authenticity of our
actions unless "in the corporate worship of the Christian
community, in which Christ's redeeming work is set forth
in word and sacrament, and the believing community responds in worship, prayer, and oblation"?[32] In Christian
worship "the double word is spoken—denial of the world
and affirmation of the world. Denial, in that Christ is set
forth and crucified; in him the contradiction between God
and the world is made manifest and the judgment of God
upon the world is pronounced. Affirmation, in that Christ's
victory over the world is announced, new birth for the
world is made possible, new hope for the world is assured."[33] The salvation of the world continues to be given
in the Church, and, more precisely, "at its center where,
in the word and sacraments of the Gospel, he himself can
lay hold upon us so that we may not be conformed to the
world but transformed by the renewing of our minds."[34]
Newbigin is convinced that the solution of the problem put

to Christians by secularization is to be found in the discourse of Jesus after the Last Supper. "I am not asking you to remove them from the world, but to protect them from the evil one. They do not belong to the world any more than I belong to the world. . . . I consecrate myself so that they too may be consecrated in truth" (Jn 17:15-19). According to Newbigin, "True religion for secular man is the abiding in that consecration."[35]

Dietrich Bonhoeffer

Having recalled some of the ideas expressed by the Bishop of Madras, India, we ought to say something about Dietrich Bonhoeffer, who has been made the patron of those who hold the most optimistic theses on secularization. I am convinced that there are, in the writings and testimony that he has left us, the wherewithal for appreciating the value of secularization, but also the means to avoid being carried away by it. In short, he brings us back to the significance and worth of what is singularly Christian. This is the reason why we look to him so much. We can not dispense ourselves then from recalling here, so that we give them their rightful place, some of the statements in his letters from prison which directly concern our subject.[36]

During the last months of his life in prison, Bonhoeffer was preoccupied with the question of the future of the Christian faith: what would become of it in a world fashioning itself and becoming more and more convinced that it should fashion itself without "the God hypothesis." The world of the twentieth century considers itself or wants to consider itself as having come of age, as belonging to a world in which men experience less and less need or desire to rely on another for their existence and intend to take their destiny in their own hands. In this sense particularly such men no longer seem "religious" to us. But Bonhoeffer's idea is that the "religion" which we see disappearing corresponds to a certain cultural period. Christian faith, if well understood, is no longer bound up with that age, any more than it was tied to other cultures through which it came to express itself during the course of centuries. Furthermore, it can gain in authenticity by being seen disengaged from the compromises of a religious attitude which is still only an all too natural expression of man. The God of revelation, the God of Gospel, shows himself as radically different from the God of "religion."

> This is the decisive difference between Christianity and all religions. Man's religiosity makes him look in his distress to the power of God in the world; he uses God as a *Deus ex machina*. The Bible however directs him to the powerlessness and suffering of God; only a suffering God can help. To this extent we may say that the process we have described by which the world came of age was an abandonment of a false conception of God, and a clearing of the decks for the God of the Bible, who conquers power and space in the world by his weakness. This must be the starting point of our "worldly" interpretation.[37]

Bonhoeffer's purpose is then not only to make it possible for men who have actually become non-religious or secular to have faith in Jesus Christ. His concern is not primarily with adaptation. First of all, he intended, by freeing Christian faith of a certain religious vesture, to bring to light what it really is and to make the God to whom it responds better known. Earlier, attention was called to his concern that we see Christ as more than "an object of religion," as belonging to a more or less limited and more and more deserted portion of the reality in which the existence of men finds expression. He wants Christ to be what He really is, "something quite different, in deed and in truth the Lord of the world."[38] Likewise, he would not want faith to take refuge in a world completely confined to "religion"; he wants it to vitalize the whole of existence. "The religious act is always something partial, faith is always something whole, an act involving the whole life."[39]

Here we have the reason why Bonhoeffer insists on the importance of the Old Testament. It keeps Christian faith rooted in the realities of the world and of history, prevents it from seeking salvation through an evasion of those realities—which could justifiably be viewed as the result of alienation. About the faith of the New Testament itself, he says, "I should like to speak of God not on the borders of life but at its center. . . . The 'beyond' of God is not the beyond of our perceptive faculties. God is the 'beyond' in the midst of our life. The Church stands not where human powers give out, on the borders, but in the center of the village."[40] In his last letters from prison, Bonhoeffer becomes less directly an advocate of secularization than a witness to a Christianity resolutely incarnate, faithful to the world and to a God whose transcendence reveals itself in a mysterious nearness to the men whom He loves.

The "Protestant Principle"

The authors whose statements we have been recalling are all Protestants. It is a fact that the theological analysis of secularization, in the exact terms in which it has been recapitulated here, has been chiefly their work from the start. The reflections in the Catholic world that would come closest to approximating this analysis are doubtless those concerned with "the relationship between the spiritual and the temporal." These held an especially prominent place in French Catholicism during the first half of the twentieth century. Some day it would be interesting to initiate a comparison between these two lines of research, the viewpoints and vocabulary proper to each.

Catholic theologians too have clearly not avoided coming up against the phenomenon of secularization, which
their Protestant colleagues have tackled head on. They
could not fail to recognize it as just as much their problem,
and some have carried on analyses, not without profiting
from the reflections and suggestions provided by the authors
referred to here. However, it seems impossible not to
recognize a link between certain ways of grappling with the
problem and the confessional tradition within which it is
conducted. Friedrich Gogarten himself never fails to refer
to the doctrine of justification by faith alone without the
works of the Law. The Baptist origins of Harvey Cox have
made him inclined to apologize for an extremely differentiated Church with structures that have no other laws than
the laws of life.

The principles of *Sola Fide,* of *Sola Gratia,* and of *Soli
Deo Gloria* put forward by the Reformation already represented a desire for disengagement (with the risk of becoming abstract) from all the Christian realities clothed in the
external forms of the world. Of these, only the Bible was
to retain an absolute value. Only its authority would remain undisputable. It was the one check to the progressive
emancipation of the believing conscience. The problem of
secularization in contemporary Protestantism is most acute
in relation to the Bible. It finds expression in the progressive tendency to hand over Sacred Scripture to the power of
an entirely independent science of criticism. In this connection, many Protestant communities are undergoing a
crisis and are suffering extremely severe tensions. Even if
the question involved is situated in a limited sphere, it always amounts to the same thing: how are we to do justice
to the autonomy proper to the world and to human reason,
which seeks to understand and organize the world, and yet
do so in such a way that not only is God not denied, but
His presence and His authority remain really witnessed to

within the world as an intimate part of human history.

Yet, even within a rather liberal Protestantism, a Paul Tillich, while constantly giving value to the "Protestant principle" of criticism and transcendence, puts no less emphasis on the view that Christian faith can be expressed only by beginning with the "structure" or "form" (*Gestalt*) of grace, starting with that "basic sacramental reality" given with Christ. We have seen too that Karl Barth, who carried to the extreme the difference between Christian revelation and faith and every other form of "religion," ends up, however, by defining Christianity as "the sacramental area created by the Holy Spirit, in which the God whose Word became flesh, continues to speak through the signs of His revelation."[41] For him too Christianity is realized concretely in the visible Church. Likewise, towards the end of Bonhoeffer's life, at the time when he was stressing the ministerial function of the Church which can only be itself by being "for others,"[42] he advocated the reestablishment of a kind of "discipline of the secret" aimed at "protecting the Christian mysteries from profanation."[43] In other words, the Church, like Christian life, while being as open to the world as one can or ought to conceive, always postulates an interiority, or what Bonhoeffer calls its own "space."

Doubtless, this special "space," without which no reality can truly be conceived in our world, is not measured in exactly the same way by different Christian confessions. The Catholic faith testifies to the conviction that God, in Jesus Christ, is involved not only in the word but also in the hierarchical and sacramental institution that constitutes the structure of the Church, the spouse and body of Christ. Likewise, the "disestablishment" with which the Church is at present unmistakably concerned in order that her spiritual reality may be evidenced more clearly could not have the same boundaries as other Christian families. The "reserve"

that she manifests in the face of the development of
secularization will normally also be greater and more assured, not necessarily because of political or social conservatism but out of fidelity to her own being.

The Church's fidelity to herself does not exclude the
necessity incumbent upon her to be always purifying herself in order that she may show forth more perfectly the
figure of her Lord. Her work of sanctification flows from
the conviction that, in order to bring to the world what she
ought to give it, the Church is not to efface herself simply
and unconditionally before the world but to keep on being
ever more and more truly herself.

This is the position taken by the Vatican Council. And
it can be said that the best efforts of Catholic theologians
went into its work.

Perspectives of the Second Vatican Council

The Council did not treat of the problem of secularization
by name. Moreover, it can be questioned whether secularization is one problem among others that are concrete reflections of contemporary theology or whether it defines the
context within which most of today's problems are to be
found. The reality to which it refers was not absent from
the thoughts of the Conciliar Fathers. It is evident in texts
such as the following in reference to atheism: "Modern
civilization itself often complicates the approach to God,
not for any essential reason, but because it is excessively
engrossed in earthly affairs."[44] In fact, the problem of
secularization provides a background for the *Pastoral Constitution on the Church in the Modern World.* It is taken
up purposely within a larger framework. In any case, the
Council communicates to us a sense of searching rather
than of having ready-made solutions.

This sense of searching seems apparent in the doctrine of
the Church as "a kind of sacrament, that is, at once the

sign and means of intimate union with God and of unity with all mankind";[45] of the Church as the place of Passover, in the sense of the passing of God into the world and of the world into God. This doctrine is expressed first in *Lumen Gentium, The Dogmatic Constitution on the Church*, which deals more directly with the Church in its internal structures and mysterious reality; but it is taken up again in *Gaudium et Spes*, which in some way defines the basis for the doctrine.

It can be said that the entire work of the Council was undertaken and carried on in this light. The whole aim was to examine how the Church, how Christians, can really be "signs" of God, witnessing to His reconciling presence and action without alienating or adulterating them but continuing, as their own mission implies, to give them true representation.

The Conciliar documents have obviously made only a beginning in the work that has to be done, outlining rather than definitively completing it. Much remains to be accomplished, but the direction to be taken is firmly pointed out. The static juxtaposition of faith and secularity needs to be replaced by a dynamic relationship which will permit the light and power of the faith to give a new basis to true secularity and will make it possible for secularity to maintain the transcendence of the good God and His work. While this rapport is being established, a solution to the problem of secularization will always have to be worked out anew on both the theoretical and the practical level.

It can be shown how on both levels the Council has already clearly shown us the way. In the practical sphere, has not liturgical reform set itself to move toward "a spiritual worship" in which the rites themselves "speak" in a way suited to awaken and strengthen faith so that faith, in its turn, will verify its authenticity by doing the works of God in charity? Have not all the structural reforms undertaken on different levels of the Church's life had but one

end in view—to give new life to the ecclesial body so that
it may become a true Pentecostal community, open to the
whole world, responsive to the breath of the Spirit, a community where tongues are loosened and made ready to tell
all men what their salvation is? On the theoretical plane,
the Council has furthered a more dynamic conception of
revelation, forbidden us to limit ourselves simply to protecting it by hiding it under a bushel basket, but invited us, on
the contrary, to mobilize all the resources of the human
spirit in order to make it in very truth the light of the world.
Examples could be multiplied of these beginnings of a response to the proddings of secularization.

The Council has initiated a frank dialogue with today's
world, in which secularization, like socialization, is one of
its obvious characteristics. A vital exchange has been
established, taking place within an accepted difference, to
the benefit, in all likelihood, of both the participating parties.

In fact, like every reality in the world, Christian faith can
have meaning only by demonstrating quite clearly what it is
not and by manifesting in some way its special character,
its singularity. As theologians who defend secularization
rightly remind us, the world can escape from the idolatry,
the divinization of its own powers, its own laws, and its
own values only in face of the revelation of God's sanctity.
Faith expresses itself precisely in the acknowledgement and
the "confession" of God's sanctity under the form in which
it is presented to us and by which the form of our faith
is defined.

The particular form that Christian faith must necessarily
take in the world, if it is to retain its meaning, is only partially and secondarily entrusted to us to mold. First and
fundamentally, it is given in that concrete and, at the same
time, mysterious figure in which God Himself is shown and
given to us. Every challenge to idols, to everything bogus-
holy can only be done in the *name,* that is, according to

the identity and by virtue of the good God. For Christians that name is Jesus Christ. It is the concrete figure of Jesus Christ, spoken of all throughout Scripture, recognized and interpreted by the Church, that provides Christian faith with its necessary criterion. Through Him alone can there take place any discernment of the spirits that are always at work in the world. Through reference to His unique and unfathomable figure Christianity affirms both its singularity and its radical transcendence. Even in a secularized world, there could be no question of Christians fading into an anonymity that would alienate them from what gives ground and authenticity even to their service of mankind. Their concern, like the whole Church's, must be nothing else than to become ever more perfectly configured to the mien of Him from whom they hold their name, that is, their identity. The constitutive, essential structures of what can indeed be called their "religion" are ordered to this mysterious work. That is why these structures and acts will always be invested with an inalienable function.

The progress of secularization moves Christians not to fall silent or to become disinterested in their specific character as Christians but, on the contrary, to confirm and deepen it. They must understand forward-moving secularization as a new demand upon them.

The attitude postulated for them is not of simple and generous service to the world, and still less of withdrawal into an existence foreign to that of other men. Their faith must rather be a "form" of life, faithfully molded by the Word of revelation and the sacraments of the Church, requiring them to remain in the common city which is being built, as a reminder of God's sovereign claims and the ever-to-be-discovered sign of His liberating work.

CHAPTER 5

Is There a Christian Atheism?

THE MOST EXTREME VIEW REACHED IN REGARD TO SECU-
larization is surely represented by what is called the
"death of God" theology. Much confusion still exists as to
its nature and extent. To begin by clearing these up seems
useful.[1]

Confusions to Avoid

It is unfair to include works such as those of Dietrich
Bonhoeffer, Harvey Cox, and James A. T. Robinson under
the heading of the "death of God" theology.

In Bonhoeffer's last letters from prison a point of departure can be found, it is true, for certain ideas developed
by the new death of God theologies. In this connection, we
can recall his ideas on the world "coming of age" and thinking, feeling, and working while finding it feasible to get
along without the "God hypothesis." Then, too, people
have been able to make the most of his suggestion that non-
religious interpretation of biblical ideas is necessary. Nevertheless, it is without a doubt misleading to isolate these
lines of inquiry, often presented in the form of questions
and, as their author underscores, in an unfinished and one-
sided form, from the whole body of his statements and
testimony.

It is just as unfair to rank Harvey Cox, as is frequently done, among the death of God theologians. It is true that the reflections on God which he offers us are rather brief and, more than that, disappointing. He is convinced that there is no need to go to battle for a concept, still less over a word, and that we can deduce what they fail to disclose. Cox judges that what matters is practical fidelity to the injunctions of the living God of the Bible and that the way to designate Him and to talk about Him correctly will be given as an increase. But he clearly rejects a closed humanism. After having given the highest value to man's responsibility in the world, he nonetheless makes the statement that, "God is not man and man can only be really *'response-able'* when he *responds."*[2]

In *The Secular City,* without naming his colleagues who tend to reduce everything to a purely human level, he takes a position against them. And he upholds the necessity of not wiping out the boundaries between faith and unbelief. "He [God] is also not to be identified with some particular quality in man or in human reciprocity, and he is not just a confused mode of speaking about relationships between men."[3] As already pointed out, he also recognized that he himself has often made too little of the metaphysical problems involved in man's practical choices. If he thinks that for the time being he ought to limit his undertakings in theology to going more deeply into the ethical implications of the faith, he has not closed the door on more speculative reflection on the reality of God. Or at least he refrains from making any statement that God is dead.

To include James A. T. Robinson among the death of God theologians has even less justification, especially since he has given a direct explanation of his position on the matter in his little book *Exploration into God.*[4] He even declares, "In assessment, I should have thought that the 'death of God' label was an unfortunate one."[5] And again, "the death of God is no doubt an unhappy slogan. . . ."[6] He simply thinks that it is not easy to speak aright of God and so is just reminding us of a first axiom of theology. He recognizes the pitfalls of language. He also knows that certain current representations have led many of our contemporaries to believe that God is a being who has a place only where every reality that they know and which claims their interest comes to an end. His purpose then is to reinstate God at the center of reality as grounding it and never ceasing to address it. It is up to others to decide whether or not Robinson has succeeded in what he set out to do.

To keep from stretching the concept of the death of God theology to the point where it becomes almost meaningless, the designation ought to be reserved for a certain number of ventures, chiefly American, which formally call into question the very reality of God, while at the same time paradoxically claiming to be developments of Christian thought. The directions which they take are far from convergent. At least all take for granted the end of any belief in God. Even if the intrinsic value of these theologies is open to question, even if they seem already to have reached the high point of their success—and publicity was not without a part in achieving that—the fact still remains that they have had an impressive echo. Through them we come up against one unquestionably important aspect of the state of contemporary human and Christian consciousness.

Calling the Idea of God into Question

For many men today, in fact, and among them a far from negligible number of Christians, the idea of God is being called into question and that under several headings.

First, under the heading of its possibility. The metaphysical universe, that is, the system of realities different from those of actual or possible human existence has defin-

itively broken down, it is said. The "transcendental illusions" analyzed by Kant are, at the present time,
recognized in a sort of spontaneous way as illusions.
Some kind of positivism has become the ordinary way of thinking for twentieth century minds: a positivism founded at
the start on scientific culture, directed to knowing and
mastering natural phenomena; a positivism proceeding
from a critique of language denying any significance to
statements not based on experience; a neo-positivism
represented by the structuralist current of thought, which
tends to see the different manifestations of human reality
from the sole point of view of the relations maintained
among its constituent elements. In the last instance, to the
elimination of every idea of transcendence is often added
an insistence on the discontinuities in the movement of history. The idea of God is regarded as the keystone of a
cultural system now vanished.

Next, what of the utility of the idea of God? Besides being impossible, it seems that it is useless too, as the most
elementary experience will verify. A man who believes in
heaven and a man who does not can both reach the same
concrete decisions. To put it another way, referring things
to heaven plainly has no efficacy. Don't religious ideas, it
is asked, always intervene to consecrate decisions already
made? Are they not like trademarks which, during the
course of history, have been put on all kinds of merchandise?
Opposing armies, we know, have often, in the name of the
same God, defended radically different interests and even
values. Observations like these, which everybody can make,
seem more and more confirmed in our day at a scientific
level by history, sociology, and, in general, the human
sciences.

However, although at first this may seem contradictory,
the idea of God is also readily declared harmful to the precise degree to which it tends to "conserve" the established

order by furnishing it with a transcendent justification, thus revealing itself as essentially conservative and negative in regard to liberty and creativity. It reflects a hierarchical order, foreordained and paternalistic, a system of accepting no matter what. It has imprisoned man inside a "sacred" structure, not to be touched but to be endured. The idea of God is a principle of alienation. By orienting man to a "beyond" and to a "world hereafter," it moves him to commit his destiny to someone outside himself, to renounce becoming himself by humanizing his world.

Such ideas, systematically developed by Marxism, following Feuerbach, and by Nietzsche, and some forms of existentialism as well, have become almost commonplace and are apt to be accepted by many people as evident.

The "Death of God" Theologies

It is within this historical-cultural context that the theologies called "death of God" stand out. They claim to record the general suspicion that weighs down heavily on the idea of God among their contemporaries or its pure and simple disappearance from their horizons. Their representatives see this as the final word in a definitively achieved secularization and make an effort somehow to baptize the actual situation.

Thomas Ogletree has given us a penetrating study, both sympathetic and lucidly critical, of the principal American representatives of this theology.[7] There is no question of reproducing the content of his fine analyses here. It will be enough to see the death of God theologies as the most radical attempt in our time to detach Christianity from all its former cultural ties in order to make it entirely responsive to the work of human advancement and world development.

The Christianity advocated by Gabriel Vahanian has nothing but iconoclastic or image-breaking content, that is, in reality, a rejection of every transcendent determination. But can what is in no way determined still have reality for us? Moreover, in that case, theological reflections quite naturally adopt the simple form of giving a reading of different manifestations of human, profane culture.

For William Hamilton, faith is expressed on the whole as a way of serving as a "lieutenant" for the Gospel Jesus. The task of the Christian is to "unmask" the Jesus hidden in the world and "to become" Jesus in and for the world. Faith becomes real always and only in the framework of temporal existence, for example, in the struggle, shared with all generous men, for civil rights and against racism and injustice in every form.

Paul Van Buren interprets Christian faith after the death of God as an experience of liberty, a liberty powerfully affirmed in the person, the words, and the whole conduct of Jesus. It communicates its "contagion" to the Christian, takes hold of him, possesses him. In turn, this liberty immediately projects the believer into the realities of the world where it becomes embodied.

As for Thomas Altizer, he sees in the doctrine of the incarnation and of kenosis a justification for absorbing everything sacred and every trace of transcendence into the profanity of the world. When the Word became flesh, he maintains, His preincarnate and originally sacred form was completely obliterated. In the incarnation so interpreted, God despoils himself of transcendence and of the abstract character of his preincarnate form: He is dead, He is no longer "other," strange and empty, relegated to the isolation of heaven, incapable of being affected by human becoming. Transcendence becomes real by being changed into complete immanence. The presence of God—if it is possible to continue to speak in that way—is essentially given in an instant, in *our* present, in *our* time, in *our* existence. Our living can thus be called "an epiphany of the body of Christ."

These theologies, allied as they are with different philosophies—a rather vague agnosticism in Hamilton, logical positivism in Van Buren, avatar of Hegelianism in Altizer —thematize or aim to contribute a speculative foundation to a conception of Christianity which, as we must recognize, is rather widespread today: a "horizontal" Christianity, as it is sometimes designated, which pours itself out entirely in an undefined idea of serving the world and mankind. It has been characterized as summed up in the principle, "Be good to one another." The death of God theologians in general have frankly admitted that the Christianity which they propose breaks with every form accepted in the past and has no ties with any existing church. The theology which they are elaborating makes no claim of belonging to any confession or of entailing any normative value whatsoever. At the university, it is listed with the religious sciences as an objective exploration and inquiry into the question of tradition. It refuses to recognize the unique character of the Bible or of the authority of the Church's word.

Christology without a Basis

The death of God theologians, or at least the last three just quoted, are of particular interest because they quite explicitly base their interpretation of Christianity on the historical figure of Jesus of Nazareth. The liberal theology of the nineteenth century, as has been remarked, tended to absorb Christology into theology because Jesus seemed to present more difficulties than God; Christianity seemed to be able to demonstrate its meaning only within a "religious experience." The new "radical" theologies have exerted themselves to absorb theology into Christology, or more precisely, into "Jesusology," starting from the idea that it is the reality of God and the very notion of religion which create difficulty. Altizer even bases his speculation on the opposition between oriental mystiques and Christian faith. In one way or another, he explains, what is sought is the *coincidentia oppositorum,* the coincidence of contraries, of the sacred and the profane. While in oriental mysticism coincidence is achieved by the absorption of the profane into the sacred, in Christianity it is effected by the sacred entering into and even disappearing within the profanity of the world. According to him this would be the true sense of the incarnation.

However, in the one-sided form in which these theological essays are developed, they can only end in the quasi-total dissolution of Christianity, even more surely than the projects alluded to earlier, which, taking the opposite tack, tend to overlook the historical anchorage of the faith. If the death of God theologies still have meaning, and I think, in spite of everything, Christian meaning, if they can still, in a paradoxical way, lay claim to the title of *theological* works, it is because, with more or less inconsistency, they accord to Jesus of the Gospels not only an exceptional, but an apparently decisive, significance. For their representatives, Jesus becomes a veritable principle of existence and, in some way, an absolute point of reference. They tend to reinvest in Him the content of the idea of God, as Ogletree has noted and judiciously reflected upon. Whence comes the call to "lieutenancy" heard by Hamilton, the power of liberty that seized Van Buren; and who confers upon a moment of time the weight of eternity that Altizer perceives in it, if Jesus is not or ceases to be the living and ever present Word of a God who, while being involved in time, absolutely dominates it, does not empty Himself into it but "dwells eternally" in it, a God revealing Himself in time precisely as eternal? What is it that makes it possible for us not to submit ourselves exclusively, as we might actually do, to the law of time, not to be content with the fullness of the

moment but to be instead a critical presence in the universe
of time capable of giving it direction and meaning, if it is
not the sustained recognition that its principle and end are
to be found in itself and, at the same time, beyond itself,
in Him who founds and redeems it? It is true that, by His
Incarnation, God allows Himself to be met in the concrete
state of our temporal existence. But this affirmation would
lose its whole foundation if Jesus were just a man among
other men, a simple link, however brilliant, in the chain
of history. If, for Christians, He is the absolute point of
reference, it is because He Himself is recognized as the
Absolute. If His word is received with interest and ad-
miration and if those who believe in Him stake their whole
lives upon Him, it is because "there has never been anybody
who has spoken like Him" (Jn 7:46). If His words give
sure guidance, liberty, and life, it is because they proceed
from someone with authority, as the contemporaries of
Jesus recognized (Mt 7:29). If Christ is worthy to receive
our faith, it is because, as we know, "in His body lives the
fullness of divinity . . ." (Col 2:9).

The inconsistent venture of the death of God theologians
gives us warning that the uniqueness, the singular character,
of Christianity does not consist only in its reference to a
particular and unique figure in history but also in the recognition that in this figure all things find their absolute meaning.

CHAPTER 6

Do Some of Us
Worship the Future?

IN THE FINAL STAGE OF THE QUICK TOUR THAT WE HAVE
undertaken along some particularly significant avenues of
contemporary Christian thought, we ought to take up again
a theme that has had repercussions which, in themselves,
would be enough to make us stop to consider it: the theme
of the future. In fact, if a certain number of our contemporaries, Christians included, have the impression of finding
themselves reflected in the death of God theology, others
are more attracted by a theology of hope and of the future.

It has been remarked quite a few times that our civilization, unlike most of those preceding it, is resolutely oriented
to the future, is disturbed and fascinated by the future. It
is not to the old, laden with the weight of experience, that
people turn to learn wisdom, but to the young, the bearers
of tomorrow's secrets. Now, for a certain number of contemporary theologians, the theme of the future is not just
one among others in Christian thought but its central, if not
unique, theme. This is particularly the case with Jürgen
Moltmann, the most famous representative of this current
of theological thinking. To recall his principal theses will
suffice to stimulate our thinking.[1]

A Theology of Hope

Israel encountered God's truth in the form of promise, Moltmann explains, and we too always meet it in the same form. Eschatology (that is, relationship to the end of time) is a constitutive dimension of faith. Now it must not be brought down—as it is, for example, in Bultmann—to a simple instantaneous relation with God which will always be at the limit of time. In the preaching of Jesus and in the testimony of primitive Christianity, eschatology is expressed on the "horizontal" plane of human time. That is why theology, as the interpreter of this fundamental structure, is the "science of hope," "a knowledge in terms of hope, and to that extent . . . a knowledge of history and the historic character of truth," which is given in an "apocalypse" and not in an "epiphany."[2] According to Moltmann, the essential difference between biblical faith and other kinds of religion is not only that it refers to the God of revelation and not to the gods of nature; the difference arises even more precisely from the disparity between the God of promise and the gods of epiphany.

In opposition to Bultmann, Moltmann says that the theme of the future is "the one real problem in Christian theology."[3] It is not proposed or defined exclusively by the historical existence of the believer who must come to a decision by projecting himself forward toward what is not yet, by thus making it come to pass. It is written into the core of the object of faith, into Christology. The resurrection of Jesus especially, on which Moltmann bases his theology of hope, is an event that opens out in time and never stops referring to the future. The first witnesses of the faith make this plain. At the same time that they were declaring the resurrection of Christ as already accomplished, they were expressing an ardent expectation of His "return." There need be no fear of speaking of "the future of Jesus Christ."[4] Because Christian theology is centered on Christ's future, it must be presented fundamentally as a theology of hope. *Spes quaerens intellectum,* hope seeking understanding, could serve as its motto.

Hope is, by its nature, active. "The theologian is not concerned merely to supply a different interpretation of the world, of history, and of human nature, but to transform them in expectation of a divine transformation."[5] Christian faith, according to Moltmann, is developed, explicated, and made effective in mission. He proposes a "hermeneutics of Christian mission," that is, an interpretation of biblical testimony within the framework of the history of mission.[6] Christian testimony is given by an "Exodus community,"[7] a community that has no eternal city in this life but looks for one in the life to come (Heb 13:13-14). As God's promises are fulfilled, they attest to His fidelity and prompt Christians to action. God is always calling them to go forward. If they remain faithful to their vocation, they are in the world as a leaven of renewal at the same time that they are proclaiming the crossing of the last frontiers of the world in the resurrection of the dead.

The brief resume of Moltmann's theology of hope gives an inkling of how well suited it is to attract a generation radically dissatisfied and impatient to be done with a world which seems to them as dehumanized as it is thoroughly organized. Moltmann reminds those who have had doubts that Christianity still has something to say to us today, that it could be a most powerful principle of renewal, if not of revolution: "iron in the pale blood of Christians" in the words of a subtitle of an article in the German weekly *Der Spiegel* dedicated to current theology.[8] *The Theology of Hope* is an answer to the great work of the Marxist nonconformist Ernst Bloch entitled *Das Prinzip Hoffnung.*[9] Moltmann even aimed to show that Christian hope, founded on "a new creation of all things by the God of the resurrection of Jesus Christ,"[10] outstripped, in a sense, all atheistic revolutionary ideas. The latter, in fact, in their very pretension, bear within themselves the "seeds of resignation" since they accept in principle a human existence that they content themselves with wanting to adapt and improve, in anticipation of a reconciliation with it. Christian hope calls into question this existence itself, in the expectation of the new being promised in the resurrection of Christ.

Concern with Effectiveness

Christianity is concerned not only with looking forward to the future but is determined to work for it and so show that it conforms to a trend of our times. Throughout Anglo-Saxon countries there exists an obvious preoccupation with exorcising a faith that would have the appearance of being *irrelevant,* that is, without impact, any hold, on reality. It makes us think of what it would be like to have to do with a Christianity that would simply lend color to life or take the form of an ideology and nothing more, a system of ideas suspended somewhere above mankind, having nothing to do with their work-worn hands and no interest for their empty stomachs.

Concerns of this kind are not only legitimate; they are in harmony with at least one essential aspect of Christian truth. Jesus Himself declared, "It is not those who say to me, 'Lord, Lord,' who will enter the kingdom of heaven, but the person who does the will of my Father in heaven" (Mt 7:21). In the same sense, Jesus can say that He is "the true Vine" and that "whoever remains in me, with me in Him, bears fruit in plenty" (Jn 15:1, 5).

It is possible, if not probable, that the Christian faith, after having been closely associated with social institutions and having exercised a direct function within them, will need to take care that, in the context of secularization, it is not relegated to the margin of everything, there to find itself, in a sense, alienated. It must discover new ways of being effective. From that point of view, all the discussions going on about the idea of a "theology of revolution" need not seem the expression of unreasonable, untimely or simply childish agitation, nor need they be immediately taxed with deviating from evangelical doctrine by making it appear as a sheer mystique of nonviolence. Undeniably, there is some danger that the Gospel may be appropriated for the benefit of movements that have their source in an entirely different inspiration. Yet research along these lines can also well up from an authentic concern not to let the Gospel evaporate in ethereal regions with no relationship to the lot of men and with the consequent risk of simply disappearing from their horizons.

It is noticeable and somewhat curious that today those who would like to keep the faith within its pure supernatural transcendence and, for example, shut up the priest within the domain of "sacred" functions and the interior life, are the same people who denounce the evil doings of secularization and withdraw from Christian civilization. If the Gospel retains real meaning for believers, then they must find ways to influence the world as it is today; and these ways will normally be different from what they would have been in bygone civilizations. To the extent that our civilization, marked by science and technology, is a civilization of planning and doing, of transforming and of looking to the future, the Gospel must be translated within a new framework. Since our civilization is also one of human initiative, since the Christian motif was not inscribed at the start in the institutions of our society—in brief, since what we have to deal with is a secular civilization—the faith's new mode of influence will no longer be like one designed in the context of Christianity. Then it was formed to safeguard as well as to animate that to which it was quite naturally ordered. Now it will doubtless more nearly ap-

proach the kind of influence the faith exerted in the first
centuries of Christianity, the kind that the New Testament
usually presents to us: the influence of a transforming and
—why not—in some circumstances, a revolutionary leaven.

The God "Who Is, Who Was, and Who Is to Come"

The meaning of transformation or revolution must be sufficiently defined so that the leaven under discussion can be
called Christian. And what of a transformation with absolutely no limits as to its direction, worked out to fulfillment by a purely immanent process? Would it not be de-
ceptive? Would it do anything else but verify the law of
natural dynamism? Is not the introduction of some outside or foreign reality into the mode of the happening, the
event, a condition for real newness? True novelty is always by way of something brought in, "introduced."

For that matter, if Christian faith is really an opening on
the future which, by its very essence, is not yet realized, if
it is creative of the future, an effective force for transformation, for radical newness, it is because it is founded on an
event, a happening. Moltmann knew this, since his whole
theology is meant to be established starting with the affirmation of the resurrection of Jesus Christ. Yet the fear
remains that his affirmation is still too vague, that its content may deal too exclusively with the resurrection and not
enough with Jesus Christ. As he defines it, Christianity
would again be in danger of becoming changed into an
ideology and of losing, by that very fact and through in-
fidelity to what is most essential in its initial purpose, its
impact and transforming action on the real world. The reflections included in a previous chapter on the historical
Jesus could find a new application here. They can also
continue by being brought to bear on the problematic of
the theologies of the future and of hope.

We should certainly find satisfaction in the attention given to the eschatological dimension of the faith in our era. The Second Vatican Council gave it strong emphasis, particularly in the *Dogmatic Constitution on the Church.* To this dimension corresponds an essential aspect of God in His work of revelation and salvation. It is an aspect clearly written in the biblical Word. The God of promises, the Kingdom that is at hand, the God who is coming, "the one who is to come" are essential themes of revelation. To put it in another way, we would be lacking something fundamental in the object proposed to our faith, if, to reach that object, we contented ourselves with looking back, with remembering, with commemorating or if we were simply to assume that we are already in possession of the whole truth and the fullness of life. Faith makes us look forward too. It makes us wait, call out, hope. Saint Paul beautifully expressed the threefold dimension of the faith in its central expression: the eucharistic celebration. "Until the Lord comes, therefore, every time you eat this bread and drink this cup, you are proclaiming His death . . ." (1 Cor 11:26). We find the same perspectives in the ancient antiphon for the Blessed Sacrament: *"O sacrum convivium, in quo Christus sumitur; recolitur memoria passionis ejus: mens impletur gratia et futurae gloriae nobis pignus datur."* ("O sacred banquet, in which Christ is received; the memory of His passion is renewed: the mind is filled with grace, and a pledge of future glory is given to us.") Faith relates to the God "who is, who was, and who is to come."

Yet the God who is to come and toward whom people today like to look would have no meaning for us, would be in danger of becoming confused with our own desires and purposes, if He were not identified with the God who was, who is made known to us in the Word already proffered, in the Son already manifested and given, and if He were not present with us now by His Spirit, to hasten and bring to pass that future to which we are really summoned that we may meet Him there. God, it is true, always continues to be discovered in "the signs of the times," according to the Gospel saying which the Second Vatican Council chose to makes it own. But deciphering the signs is done in the light of what has been revealed in the "fullness of time" in the figure and work of Him who is already, in all His perfection, the "new man." As another theologian, Wolfhart Pannenberg, who is solicitous to reevaluate the future dimension of faith, aptly remarks in another context, "Faith is confidence accorded the promises of God; this confidence is not made superfluous but only possible by a knowledge of them."[11]

It is to the extent to which the transforming, even revolutionary, preoccupation of the faith is always grounded anew on the revelation already accomplished in the coming Kingdom of God, it is to the extent to which our generous enterprises are inspired and measured by revelation, that we have the capacity to prevent ourselves from being carried along by the impersonal "movement of history." Thus freed, we also have the ability to introduce, and are perhaps the only ones to do so, a real and radical newness into our world. Revelation and the figure of Jesus Christ provide us with a principle of discernment which, far from closing the door to initiative, opens the way to it. Without discernment, faith that focuses on the future and is overeager to engage in transforming action, normally leads to two deadly attitudes that only seem opposed to each other: purely negative and anarchical contention and the pursuit of a utopia, a kind of millenium.

After having given a sympathetic exposition of Moltmann's theology of hope, Heinz Zahrnt puts his finger on its deficiencies, which Moltmann himself has subsequently partly supplied: "But the emphasis laid on the future by many theologians at present is so exaggerated that it becomes suspicious."[12] God can be driven just as far away from reality by overaccenting His futurity as by holding to an ill-conceived transcendentalism. In both cases, man looks for Him and can no longer find Him in a concrete form. To a world which increasingly understands itself more as a task to be accomplished than as a gift to be received, Christian faith can bring its contribution only by cleaving to and being taught by the original Word and figure that confer upon it its own unique character, its singularity.

PART TWO

WITHIN THE
REALM OF FIGURES

CHAPTER 7

A Historical Religion

NOWADAYS IT IS NOT AT ALL UNCOMMON FOR PEOPLE TO speak of Christianity as a historical religion. It has not always been so. When historical science, in its first triumphant ventures, set out to survey Christianity within the compass of its categories and schemas in order, as it were, to "master" it, apologists were more willing to speak of Christianity's "truth" than of its historicity. If "historical" was opposed to, or seemed opposed to, "absolute," to recognize Christianity's historicity could appear as an admission of weakness.

The same apologists continued, it is true, to defend the "historicity" of statements made in the Bible, particularly those about extraordinary occurrences which the science of historical criticism held in suspicion. But in both cases, historicity was at that time immediately identified with truth: this demonstrates how ambiguous the concept of "historical" is and how real is the need for it to be clarified when talking about the historicity of Christianity.

The purpose here is not to engage in a study of the concepts of history and historicity considered in themselves but to return as directly as possible to the nature of Christian specificity. It does seem that it must be first grounded in the historicity of its object and there find its first expression.

The Judeo-Christian Innovation

By qualifying Christianity as historical, it is not enough to say that Christianity takes form within the realities of history among other realities to be found in the world and that, in other words, it is not solely an interior, hidden reality, a secret or fleeting disposition of the soul which would only affect or be known by the individual concerned. Nor is it enough to add that Christianity finds expression in a visible Church that has followed a verifiable course through the passage of centuries. Certainly all of this is affirmed, but there is still something more fundamental that can be expressed more precisely. For all the great religions of the world are, at least up to a certain point, historical religions in a general sense.

What fundamentally specifies Christianity is that it defines a faith essentially founded on history, based on a revelation not only given in history but which is itself history, a revelation that unfolds in time, that is the concrete molding process of a particular people and that culminates in a historical person and destiny.

Christian faith is not a celebration of nature, its cycles, its fertility, or its "mysteries." It speaks of an initiative, of a principle that discloses itself not as an immanent source of energy but as a creative liberty, an original subjectivity. It is not come across as *toujours-là,* as always there, but encountered as an event. Such is the sense that the idea of revelation assumes in biblical faith.

Biblical faith is not a direct communication of a knowledge of "things" not accessible to natural intelligence; of "things" which would be basically of the same nature but could only be introduced by other means; of "things" that one can accept only, as it were, by making a recording of them because they are taught and can only be taught, in contrast to those "things" that we can come to discover and to "establish" by ourselves. It is true that the "mysteries" of the faith have often been presented in this way: as "truths" to accept, even if there is "nothing to understand." As a result, criticism is sparked by the very idea of a truth that we can make our own without recognizing it as such, that is, without interiorizing it.

To be real, revelation has to be known, assimilated. The transcendent or, if you will, supernatural character of the revelation to which Christian faith relates is due to the fact that it does not come into being on the basis of what is already given, even implicitly or "in potency," but by way of an absolute beginning, as something radically new.

This does not mean that, as Bultmann advocates, we ought or can reduce revelation to pure factuality, to a simple *Dass*, a simple "fact that" without determinate content. An absolute beginning, a radical innovation, it is the commencement of *something*, the genesis of a whole new world of existence and thought, in the words of St. Paul, "a new creation" (2 Cor 5:17). Yet this new world, this new creation, comprehends and preserves its true nature only to the extent that it does not separate itself from the original act, the personal initiative which brought it into being.

Thus Christian faith, following upon the Jewish faith, relates fundamentally to a novelty. To admit the possibility of that is a basic condition for faith. To confess, magnify, and then promote this innovation is to express it. This newness firmly asserted in the New Testament took a deep hold on the Christian people of the first few centuries, but became less perceptible during that whole long period when Christianity, having become the principal bond of human society, came all too easily to seem to be something ordinary or normal or, even more than that, to be the mainspring of conservatism. This occurred in spite of the fact that constant checks of criticism and unwearying calls for reform always kept reminding it of its irreducible origin. We, in our day, should be in a better position to perceive and proclaim the real newness that Christian faith holds out to the world. It not only opens up amazing possibilities contained within the vital energies and, above all, in the intelligence of man, but it creates a new status for humanity, according to the efficacious purpose of Him who has called existence out of nothingness, raised the dead to life and made all things new.

To say that Christianity is new is also to say that it is essentially original as well. Its specificity is not the same as the trait possessed by all existent things to distinguish one from another and prevent them all from being lost in universal confusion. The specificity or singularity of Christianity is its very nature and belongs not only to its origin but to its every concrete manifestation.

A Working God

One quality of this innovation is that it does not "settle down." If it did, it would grow old. It is a continual passing from the old into the new. The most obvious testimony to this structure of the object of faith is the Bible itself with its division into the Old and New Testaments and the dynamism leading from the one to the other. One of Dietrich Bonhoeffer's merits is that he insisted upon the importance of this fundamental structure and spoke of it again and again when talking about the "last things" and the "things-before-the last," accenting the necessity of not betraying "the old" and the "things-before-the last." In this way he wanted to ensure the real historicity of a faith that seemed to him in need of complete rethinking. God's initiative, in fact, grounds its whole historical realism in not being content with making itself known as "behind" the events of human history, as if it were a transcendental idea, but by being written right into history. God's initiative is not implied by the faith at the limit of temporal history;

it operates effectively within history and is offered as knowledge to those to whom it is communicated. Thus it traverses the history of a people whom, according to the Bible, it never gave up pursuing and regaining over and over again through a thousand ups and downs along ways ever new. It has retained the innovative quality that it had from the start. Moreover, those whom it once touched always continued to be confounded by it until the day when it appeared in the absolute manifestation of the New Adam, wholly engendered by the creator Spirit. In that day, the majority of the people who had until then served as its receptacle found it impossible to accept and broke away from it.

However, the radical innovation wrought in the advent of the Son of God continues to be written in the depths of history. It is not communicated like a bolt of lightning or hidden under a mask. From the time of its origin, the Christian Church has had to combat the idea that faith has to do with a mere *appearance* of God's presence in the flesh and in history. Docetism would destroy both the reality of the incarnation and the innovative force that it introduced. Conceived by the Holy Spirit, the Son of God is also the son of a woman. A work of grace, of the divine loving kindness, Jesus is nonetheless a fruit of our earth. *Dominus dedit benignitatem et terra nostra dabit fructum suum* ("The Lord has shown His kindness, and our earth will bear its fruit"): the liturgy can apply the verse from Psalm 85 to the mystery of Christmas.

From the beginning, the revealing and saving initiative of God and the force of innovation that it introduced into the world have been interpreted as a real work of God. Jesus could say, after healing the sick man by the pool of Bethzatha, "My Father goes on working and so do I" (Jn 5:17). From the same viewpoint, the Fathers of the Church developed the theme of a divine pedagogy, of a work of education by which God prepared His people to receive, to support and to understand Him who was to utter the fullness of His Word and to accomplish all justice. How would it have been possible for Jesus to announce the coming of the Kingdom, to get people to understand the nature of the "justice" that He was accomplishing, to disclose the mission and the shocking fate of the "Servant" and the "Son of Man," if these concepts, together with many others, had not first been forged and, above all, filled with concrete meaning, throughout a long history? The Word of God accomplished in Jesus Christ, the creative Word of meaning and of radical innovation, beginning with the wholly gratuitous initiative of God, is true speech, espousing the laws of human discourse and acquiring throughout time a veritable body of expression.

The whole Bible, especially the Old Testament, witnesses to God's work, to His patience, His long-suffering, and the trouble He takes. The newness of God's revealing initiative discloses itself at its height, although in a paradoxical form, in the unexpected guise in which He presents Himself to us. Far from displaying His magnificence by manipulating the laws of human and historical reality, He espouses them with immeasurable seriousness to the point of having His glory shine out on us from the disfigured features of the Servant and in the ignominy of the cross. Tertullian's *credo quia absurdum,* "I believe because it is absurd," does not simply express a pious exaggeration; it conveys the experience of a believer who recognizes the completely novel character of what God has revealed of His work and of Himself.

However—as a sort of redoubling of the paradox—the revelation of God *in contrario,* as Luther (perhaps too one-sidedly) liked to qualify it, presents itself to us at the same time as superlatively creative of meaning. And the manifestation, articulation, and explanation of that meaning forms an integral part of revelation. Revelation is history, disconcerting history, an ever-new production. It is also prophecy.

As seen in and by the Bible, prophecy is not, as we know, identified with divination or with the simple advance announcement of anticipated future events. These would be at the most secondary, derivative, and possibly debased forms of true prophecy. Prophets are something quite different from diviners and have understood their mission as different. They are men to whom the Spirit of God gives the perception to discover, in situations or events in which they are involved, dimensions not perceived by their contemporaries and not accessible to human eyes. They are men endowed with the power to discover, in the concrete context of their era and in apparently natural happenings such as war, deportation, and famine, God's plan leading history toward its term, toward a more or less distant end where its meaning will be achieved.

That final and, in point of fact, absolute meaning is given, in conformity with the logic of historical revelation, in the uniqueness of an event that reaches the summit of paradox: a death bearing all promises and all hopes, a single "hour" laden with the weight of eternity. *Ephapax* ("once and for all"), as the Epistle to the Hebrews says it (Heb 7:27; 9:12; 10:10); or, as Bultmann aptly expresses it, "the eschatological event." He, however, did not give sufficient attention to the conditions needed to speak of a true event. Whatever his intentions, he weakens the strength of the paradox by not situating its eschatological meaning and import *in* the historical event itself, or more precisely, within historical existence, in the body of flesh in which it is lived.

The lasting and constantly renewed specificity or singularity of Christian faith is grounded in the unique point of space and time in which there took place an exchange between God and human history, and God passed over into our world and our world passed over into God.

The Faith on Trial by the Historical Sciences

To make it understood that the "historicity" of Christianity is the foundation for its specificity or, if you will, its uniqueness, is to suggest its transcendence: something is implied that cannot be compared to anything else and which, because it produces something entirely new, must be introduced from some other source. Just the same, because Christianity is written into history, it is exposed to a critical examination of what it claims to be. It comes within the province of historical science which, in modern times, has experienced extraordinary development. If the *Credo* includes a statement as precise as that a certain man suffered, died, and was buried "under Pontius Pilate," at the same time that it becomes a subject for confession it also becomes an object of human science. If this is so, is not this statement and others of the same nature in the *Credo* then going to be likened to other contingent realities broken up in the complex play of currents and influences which the historian spends his time trying to unravel? Will it not be condemned to the leveling process which science always imposes on its object because, by its very nature, it can only operate in the domain of immanence?

It is undeniable that the historical-critical consideration of Christianity and of all the realities bound up with the Christian faith has brought about a profound crisis for the faith. The conflict that frequently breaks out between science and faith is most acute in the area of history. Only there does the conflict seem to take on an inevitable character, and it cannot be laid to the account of problems poorly stated; on the contrary, it proceeds from the very nature of the Christian reality, of that paradoxical liaison sustained between divine transcendence and authentic human history. This is also why the clash between traditional faith and the historical-critical process is a choice place for discovering in what Christian specificity consists.

For some who were the first to accept the claims of historical science without reservation, it seemed at that time to be an invincible adversary of the faith. If it did not necessarily mark its end right then, it at least was going to make a radical change in its nature. It appeared that faith could only continue to exist by being relegated to the interior regions of moral inspiration, that, in any case, it could not find a basis in what comes under the judgment of science. How, asked Lessing (1729-1781), could my eternal happiness rest on the reading of a contingent event in history? Can I have my salvation depend on an enterprise which will always resemble the weaving of a spider's web? The more my instruments of analysis are perfected, the more will I grasp the really infinite complexity of the relations obtaining among the events of history—were I only able, other than by abstraction, to isolate a single event from the web of relations constituting it. Between what my critical examination permits me to read and what the faith claims to know there is a frightful abyss to cross. The existence of that "abyss" is admitted by defenders of the faith as well as by those bent on demonstrating its impossibility. The development of the theme of "sacred history" or the "history of salvation," which would belong to an entirely different order than profane history, has offered an escape from the reductions of criticisms, but it means running a great risk of making the term "history" in this instance undeserving of being so designated. The adoption of these new categories involves either starting or continuing on the way to dualism and, as a result, toward the destruction of what specifically comprises Christian uniqueness or specificity. For Oscar Cullman, the notion of salvation history is central to his theology. With some point, Bultmann could well ask him just what meaning the term *history* retains in this context. The same question always lies in wait for those who see no difficulty in dealing with the notions of "divine facts" and "supernatural events." Not that these formulas are in themselves unacceptable, but that they preserve their meaning only insofar as the nature of the tie uniting the substantive and the modifier in this expression is made clear. They run the greatest risk of ending in monophysism or docetism: whether these "facts" and "events" are considered as homogeneous with other facts and events of history, or whether their historical character is allowed to seem only apparent.

The confrontation of faith and history cannot be solved by a few noncritical statements, any more than it can be settled by a victory proclamation made by one of the parties to the dispute. Rather, it should enable us to have a better understanding of the proper object of both faith and history and of the relation between them as well.

Some liberal theologians and some apologists have sought too simple a solution to the crisis resulting from the development of historical science by looking for Christian truth in regions beyond the reach of the changing fortunes of history. Adolf Harnack (1851-1930) is the most typical representative of this kind of Christian apologetics, which really consists in severing Christianity's bonds with history. According to Harnack, the Gospel "contains something which, under differing historical forms, is of permanent validity." The essence of Christianity, according to the title of his famous work,[1] is something that must be abstracted and brought to light. And he undertook to "grasp what is essential in the phenomena, and to distinguish kernel and husk."[2] "The oftener I reread and consider the Gospels, the more do I find that the contemporary discords, in the midst of which the Gospel stood, and out of which it arose, sink into the background."[3] "God and the soul, the soul and God," the sense of the divine Fatherhood, the true

filial spirit, are what Harnack discovers after having eliminated what is passing, what is purely historical. For, if it
is true that in certain respects "the view of the world and
of history with which the Gospel is connected is quite different from ours ... 'indissoluble' the connection is not."
What is essential in the Gospel is timeless.[4] The relatively
contingent circumstances with which Christianity found itself connected enhanced the person of Jesus who announced
the Gospel. Without a doubt, His extraordinary personality
conferred on the words He spoke a special accent which
alone can explain the extraordinary way that they have
echoed and reechoed down through nineteen centuries into
our very own time. Jesus can always be considered as
"the Way to the Father," the one who gives the Gospel its force; and He continues to be for many people
much more than a simple doctrine—a living example. Yet,
to Harnack's mind, Jesus did not make Himself part of
his Gospel. "The Gospel, as Jesus proclaimed it, has to
do with the Father only and not with the Son."[5] Harnack
was unable to offer a proposal for a "dehistoricizing" of
Christianity without dechristianizing it, without taking away
from it what is its mark.

About the same time, other theologians foresaw more
clearly the nature of the "test" of truth that the development
of historical science would necessarily pose for the faith.
Ernst Troeltsch (1865-1923), one of those who tried
hardest to integrate historical inquiry within theology, made
the statement that a whole "world view" is already contained in the idea of the "purely historical," which directs a
scholar's research and evaluates each of its results. And
he was of the opinion that historical criticism, once it has
been applied to biblical science and the history of the
Church, could not fail to become a real ferment for transforming and revolutionizing former theological methods.
From a similar viewpoint, Alfred Loisy, in his controversy

with Maurice Blondel about the subject of his book
L'Évangile et l'Église, explained that all he had in mind was
to do the work of a historian or, more exactly, in opposition to Harnack, to lay the foundations for a historical
apologetic for Christianity. Besides, he did not see how
his work could contradict dogma since it did not touch
upon it but belonged to and operated within an entirely
different category.

> It does not seem to me that my book implies a
> denial of any dogma; it only implies the necessity for
> revising all theological teaching from the point of view
> of history in order to make a positive contribution to
> its truth and, from a philosophical point of view, to
> make it more intelligible theoretically.[6]

In an article on "The Significance of the Critical Historical Method for Church and Theology in Protestantism,"[7]
Gerhard Ebeling gives an exact analysis of the radical
transformation which, he thinks, is brought about in the
way in which the faith is understood simply by the application of the procedures of modern historical science, determined above all by criticism. The historical-critical
method, he explains, leads the theologian to take into consideration the different realities that have to do with the
faith and are essentially problematical, affected by the con-
tingency that specifies every historical datum whatsoever.
Also, corresponding to the use of this method, which by its
nature cannot, according to Ebeling, admit of any limita-
tion, is a quite definite understanding of the faith itself. It
is impossible for this understanding to be willing to be
based on any authority, whatever that might be, which
claims to be indisputable—for example, the Bible as literally
inspired, the Church as the mystical body of Christ, Tradition as an absolute rule of faith. It is impossible for it to

look for support in a domain which would be right and in fact escape the instability and uncertainty of things human. As a result of the historical-critical method, on the contrary, faith finds itself confronted by the radical ambiguity of any and every reality and can only be determined in this constantly renewed confrontation, and so by being definitively grounded only on itself. This new status of the faith in some way drives the believer in *Sola Fide* into a corner.

However, is it not a characteristic of a veritable historical faith not to be "all by itself," but to be specified by the singularity of an object which is not history in general and still less that sort of abstraction called historicity, but by an "object," a reality that has "taken place," that refers to a particular point in space and time? Without any anchorage in a specific event, faith necessarily tends, as remarked earlier, to be confused with the spontaneous activity of human reason. Would Christian faith then be just another name for a contemporary rationalism?

The Crisis of History

Faith is not alone in experiencing a crisis as the result of the development of the critical method. Historical science too has passed through one that touches its very purpose. The crisis was to revive, to a considerable degree, the problems with which the eighteenth and nineteenth centuries had tried to deal.

It is increasingly evident that the aim to get back to the "purely historical" is a false hope. Defining the historical task as simply the careful establishment of "how things really happened" (*wie es eigentlich gewesen,* according to Ranke's famous formula) belongs to an obviously inadequate, if not a misleading, conception of history. This is increasingly the case as the object involved is richer and more concrete, when it is a matter of a historical reality in the full purport of that term and not just a date or some detail with no intrinsic significance. One of Pirandello's characters says that a fact is like a sack: it stands up only if you put something inside it. History, in the true sense of the word, is more than a simple chronicle that does not look for the meaning of things and events. Meaning is not just that which makes it possible for us to comprehend things and events: it is also what really make them what they are.

History is always a sensible, judicious reconstruction of reality. As Raymond Aron writes, there exists no ready-made historical reality suitably prepared in advance for science to make a faithful reproduction of. Henri-Irénée Marrou, who quotes this statement, continues, "History is a result of effort and, in a sense, of a creative effort, by which a historian, the knowing subject, establishes rapport between the past which he brings back and the present that is his own."[8] Not that the historian makes up his work out of whole cloth, He discovers it; but his discovery is always active, it always involves him.

Indeed, the very object of historical understanding itself continually reminds the historian of the permanently provisional character of his research and the necessity of always looking beyond, of going farther. The smallest fact really discloses itself to him as "the starting point of a chain reaction" and, to put it properly, has no independent existence apart from its inexhaustible context. So the whole problem of any history, however limited it may be, postulates a knowledge that moves forward by degrees toward a knowledge of the whole of history; and since it is impossible to reach that, it must remain, if it is to be faithful to the reality on which it bears, incomplete, relative, and fundamentally open.

This characteristic is not just the result of the infinite and inexhaustible complexity of its object. It is also due to (the two reasons are connected) the largeness of view of the historian, that is, of the *subject* who undertakes to uncover historical reality.

The universality or generality, the validity of the concepts used by the historian [Marrou writes], are indeed, one should not say relative but dependent, not, strictly speaking, on the personality of the historian, his mentality or his times, but rather on the truth of the implicit and, to be desired, explicit philosophy that makes it possible for him to elaborate them. History does not hold up alone. Contrary to what the positivists imagine, it is a part of a whole, of a cultural organism in which man's philosophy acts as axis, frame, and nervous system; history stands or falls with the whole. We must venture to recognize the firmly structured character of knowledge and the unity binding together the different manifestations of the human mind.[9]

Along the same lines, when opposing what he termed Loisy's "historicism," Blondel recalled the solidarity of the sciences, the interdependence of all human problems, and so denied the possibility of a "separate" history.

From another point of view, starting with the fact that historical knowledge is always mediate, that it is based on the idea of testimony, and is not, therefore, susceptible of demonstration and, as a result, is not a science properly speaking, Marrou does not hesitate to characterize it as "faith knowledge." Of course, only a matter of "natural" faith is meant here. All that has just been said at least helps us to understand that, if the relationship of faith to history can present problems, no fundamental opposition between faith and history exists in every case, as the rationalism of the eighteenth and nineteenth centuries was all too quick to claim.

Furthermore, today, without repudiating any of the re-

quirements of criticism and rationality and without depriv-
ing the faith of its transcendence, approaches have been
laid out for grounding faith in history. Oscar Cullman and,
especially, Wolfhart Pannenberg have made this particular
and valuable contribution.

Profiting by the numerous criticisms made about his early
works, particularly in regard to the over-simple objectivism
of the framework within which he liked to speak of history,
Cullmann, in his important work *Salvation in History*,[10]
shows how the faith as defined by the New Testament consists in inserting the existence of the believer in a time
structured by God's intervention and given an absolute point
of reference in the manifestation of Jesus Christ.

As to Pannenberg's theology, it is and is intended to be
a whole theology of history. *Revelation as History*[11] is the
significant title given by him to a collection of articles by
different authors, to which he contributed an introduction
and an article of his own. It is reminiscent of Cullman's
work just cited. For Pannenberg, the biblical Word of revelation is conveyed within and expresses a far vaster reality.
The reality is history. The character of revelation is not
added to events but given in them. And, according to
Pannenberg, it is only in this way that they can serve as a
basis for faith. This must be so if faith intends to remain
Christian faith.

Since history is a concrete whole, as Marrou reminds us,
it is only on the basis of or within the compass of history
in general that the particular history to which revelation
testifies can find its full meaning. So Pannenberg does not
separate the history of revelation from the history of the
world as it is opened up to exploration by our critical intelligence. On the other hand, he knows that we do not
"comprehend" history as a whole, were that only because
history is not yet finished and cannot, therefore, be summed
up. Faith does not perform any such summarization; it

does, however, recognize Jesus Christ as the anticipated term of all human history. The historical fate of Jesus opens up to the believer a vista within which the meaning of all history is laid bare. Here is the enduring anchorage for the faith of a Christian and at the same time the exact ground from which his understanding of the world unfolds.

The Historical Existence of the Christian

Corresponding to the innovation introduced by the divine initiative and recognized by faith, there takes place the believer's entrance into a new existence. "And for anyone who is in Christ, there is a new creation; the old creation has gone, and now the new one is here" (2 Cor 5:17). The Christian is divested of his old self in order to be renewed in mind and thought and to put on his new self "which will progress towards true knowledge the more it is renewed in the image of its creator" (see Eph 4:24; Col 3:10).

This new thing in the life of a Christian, as well as in the universe which it penetrates, is introduced by an event: an encounter at the very core of his existence with a person who summons him to a radical reversal, a sort of inversion of his whole being, a real change of course. It is the *metanoia* spoken of by the New Testament and translated by us both as "conversion" and "repentance." "Repent, for the kingdom of heaven is close at hand" (see Mt 4:17 and parallel passages). So it was that Jesus began His mission.

The reversal brought about by the Word of God means an uprooting from a mode of existence and from a whole world characterized by the Bible as a world of sin. It is not an uprooting from human existence as such; it is not an evasion of or a flight from the world of men and its cares, troubles, and struggles. On the contrary, it is a first step on a real adventure. After calling for that conversion without

which it is impossible to enter into the kingdom of God,
Jesus does not propose that we settle down in a haven of
refuge. Instead, he asks that we "follow" him. "Follow me"
are the words with which he called His first disciples (see
Mt 4:19 and parallel passages). These are often repeated
words: "If anyone wants to be a follower of mine, let him
renounce himself and take up his cross and follow me"
(see Mt 16:24 and parallels). The theme of the *sequela
Christi,* the following of Christ, will be, we know, taken up
again and again in Christian Tradition. It is in response
to this call, particularly, that the different forms of religious
life have been worked out, including everything from the
way of life adopted by the desert Fathers to the life of missionaries, who go to the far places of the world to proclaim
the Gospel. Dietrich Bonhoeffer made the following of
Jesus the basic theme of his talks at the pastoral Seminary
of Finkenwalde. These were later collected and published in
the beautiful book perfectly expressed in its German title
Nachfolge, "the following," translated into English as *The
Cost of Discipleship.*[12]

Neither the solitaries of the desert nor the missionaries
adventuring to far-off places have ever understood the
Christian life as a refuge from the flesh and from the times
but, quite the contrary, as an unceasing combat. The experience referred to as early as St. Paul's Epistle to the
Ephesians continued as a struggle "not against human
enemies . . . but against the Sovereignties and the Powers
who originate the darkness in the world, the spiritual army
of evil in the heavens" (Eph 6:12). Christian life carried
on the combat in which Jesus Himself engaged all throughout His life until His "agony," the final attack that He conducted against the powers of darkness.

Certainly, Christian life, like Jesus' own, does not constantly assume the same dramatic character. However, it
would doubtless be good to recall more often, in these

times, that Christian life is at least ordered to conflict. There is an admitted danger in the ecumenical orientation adopted nowadays by the great Christian confessions, particularly the Catholic Church. It is involved in sympathetic openness to other religions, in truth, even to unbelief itself in order to dialogue with them. Christianity could come to seem marked only by a preoccupation with comprehending, with understanding and, at the extreme, with approaching just a noble and liberal philosophy. It runs the risk of no longer committing itself to action, to struggle, to sacrifice. Christian life is in danger of no longer costing anything. Bonhoeffer thought of this in terms of "cheap grace," that would justify everything, excuse everything. A Christianity of that kind would quickly cease to have any appeal. It would soon seem superfluous. To make a passing comment, is it not because we have lost the sense of Christianity as a combat that we have come to shape our prayers less and less on some of the Bible psalms? The idea of a difficult and militant Christianity is doubtless the truth mixed up in the reaction of some "traditional" groups in face of the doctrinal or moral liberalism attributed to the openness initiated by the recent Council. The same truth is appealed to repeatedly and all too often inopportunely by other groups called "progressive" in their struggle for justice and even, in fact, for their revolutionary enterprises. In other words, opinions differ as to the place and object of the combat. In any case, on one side or the other, the need for it seems to be given with the faith itself. Those who, for equally good reasons, reject fanaticism and concern themselves with conciliation should not forget this.

Just the same, people with this viewpoint, this reserve, are implying another truth rooted in the historical character of Christian existence. Christian faith is not an uprooting from the human condition but is lived in time and in history. It does not completely possess what it holds and

seeks to hold but goes ahead following Jesus, who is Himself called "the Way" (Jn 14:6). As a result, it maintains
or ought to maintain a sense of the unfinished, the relative,
the imperfect. It does not establish us in perfect knowledge
and perfect liberty so that we can make infallible and immediate decisions about everything. It knows that in this
world darnel and good grain are almost always mixed, and
any final judgment falls not within our competence but is
reserved for the time to come. In the midst of realities which
at first generally seem ambiguous, it keeps on trying to find
its own way and the direction in which the battle is moving.
It does not pretend to have either the first or the last word
about everything but, as it pursues its quest with unflagging
fidelity, to let the first word and the last speak to it, continue to speak to it and to say more and more.

As Bonhoeffer again so well reminds us, we live in realities that are "before-the-last," realities of time, of the body,
of work, of an unfinished world; as to the final, absolute
realities, we only believe in them. It is in realities that are
not final, within a concrete history wherein their existence
unfolds, that believers set out to find God in humility and
patience and often with hesitation. Nothing would endanger
the authenticity of their approach as much as making up
their minds, whether out of naiveté or pride, to skip some
of the stages along the way. The struggle that we have to
carry on for truth as well as for justice is not the apocalyptic
battle at time's end but the daily and constantly shifting war-
fare against the insidious evil within us and outside of us
called sin. Or rather, in the concrete form of the everyday
combat the apocalyptic battle at the end of time is already
joined.

Although the believer lives the faith in the heart of time,
immersed in the realities of a world which is not his to
dominate, he is not, in fact, the simple plaything of history
and of the forces penetrating it, a thing buffeted about by

all the winds that blow. He makes no claim, as has been said, to being able to have the first and the last word to say about everything or to pronounce a final judgment on whatever he comes across. Yet his faith does at least supply him with road signs. It indicates to him in what direction he should set out in search of the God who summons him through the events of the world and who intends to carry out His divine designs through him. Faith does not lift the believer outside of or above history so that he can look down on it and take it all in; but by binding him to a Tradition which for him means truth itself, faith makes it possible for him to situate himself, to find and recognize his place. From its base he can start his search: he can begin to speak. If he does not know everything, he at least knows with certainty that something really took place and by that happening everything is constituted, and everything can receive and reveal meaning: the manifestation of Jesus Christ, through whom and for whom all things were created and in whom all things are held together in unity (Col 1:16-17).

Thus the innovation introduced by the revelation of God in Jesus Christ gives the believer stability, assuring him of an anchorage in history. But what it stabilizes is nothing else but a journey, a journey in understanding, with its perspectives at least given, a journey of discourse and work, in the sense of those begun by God Himself intervening in our history. On the basis of the new reality that grounds and structures his faith, the believer himself becomes capable of making this new thing come to pass and of contributing not just to revealing the form of the world but to shaping it.

CHAPTER 8

Signs of the Faith

THE THREAT THAT SEEMS TO HANG OVER A CERTAIN NUM-
ber of particularly representative theological currents at
the present time is that they may end up by becoming some
sort of faceless Christianity. Or, to look at it in another
way, the question to which these different currents keep returning is the "configuration" of the Christian faith. Recalling the historical character of the object of faith and of
the existence in which it has been realized has allowed us
to get back to the basis of the need for the "configuration"
of faith. This has been done by emphasizing how the historicity of revelation not only constitutes the seal of its
gratuity and transcendence but also bring into the world
a principle of innovation and movement. On the basis of
these considerations, an attempt should now be made to
state more precisely how rapport is articulated between the
divine initiative which establishes faith and the human history within which the believer lives the faith. We should
go to the very heart of the articulation between the two so
that we can see how the essential features of the Christian
faith are constituted and developed and how, within them,
the faith continues to remain, like the revelation that founded
it, a historical reality.

A Structured Community

God's initiative, to which faith responds, is from the beginning engraved in the constitution, life, and activity of a
people. It reaches us and remains with us through the echo
it found in the people to whom it was first addressed. The
Word of God comes to us in the form of a tradition. In
our day, the Bible is considered more and more as the
depository for the history of a tradition or of a body of
traditions.[1] Although these are particular traditions, they
are at the same time ordered to manifest a universal design: the constitution of a new humanity.

The tradition of faith continues to be lived in a Church
that has been defined by the Second Vatican Council as "a
kind of sacrament or sign of intimate union with God, and
of the unity of all mankind."[2]

There is no question of going back over all the teaching on the Church as it has been passed on to us by the
recent Council. The purpose here is simply to underscore
what gives the Christian community its singular character,
its specificity. In addition, attention will be called to the
possible danger that this could be lost sight of in efforts
which fortunately aim at revivifying and developing energies all too often stifled. At the present we are witnessing
a renewal of community life. It would be advisable to look
within it to see what assures us of its ecclesial authenticity.

For too long a time the Church's authenticity was considered sufficiently established if certain structures were
present and secure. The ecclesial reality was immediately
identified with its corporate form. It was all too easy for
people to see the Church's hierarchical representation as the
Church herself, just as they came to identify the body of
Christ only with the sacramental sign. To belong to the
Church consisted essentially in acknowledging the authority
of its leaders, subscribing to its doctrine and submitting to

its discipline. An impressive figure of the Church resulted: a flawless edifice within stout walls. Those who lived inside knew everything about what they had to think and what they had to do and so formed an almost monolithic unity. Unbelievers themselves were moved to admire the solidity of the organism. It was actually said to be an image of "the perfect society." That the Church's divine character originated in her foundation was not denied but it was, as it were, transferred to the perfection of her internal structure.

In spite of her divine origin, the Church has been exposed to the danger of presenting a too exclusively human image. We really know how an entire part of the Church, and precisely the part that happens to be most visible, has yielded more than once to the temptation to go secular, to contend for power with other spheres of power, opening the doors of her sanctuary to the game of worldly interests, honors, and money.

One of the great benefits of the Second Vatican Council is that it has brought to the fore in the doctrine on the Church its mysterious depth, God's thought, His intention, which not only brought the Church into being but has never stopped working throughout the course of time to permeate her and determine her authentic reality. The first chapter of *Lumen Gentium* deals entirely with this hidden dimension of the ecclesial mystery. It reminds us that the first principle of the existence and continuance of the Church, of her unity and her strength, is not the perfection of her organization but the Holy Spirit at work in the hearts of believers. With the same thought in mind, the second chapter of the *Constitution* does not begin with a consideration of the Church as a society defined by its structures and laws but as a society of people brought together by the same call, responding to the same vocation. Today people are more and more inclined to consider the Church as a communion.

The doctrinal report presented to the Episcopal Synod of
1969 by the Prefect of the Sacred Congregation for the
Doctrine of the Faith was also developed entirely on the
theme of the Church as communion.

The idea of communion implies interiority, intimacy, in-
terpenetration. To say that the Church is a communion is
to say that her most fundamental reality is not to be found
in the sphere of structures but in persons and in the spiritual
bond uniting them that goes by the name of charity. Whence
comes the concern shown almost everywhere today to see
the Church being expressed more and more in the form of
real communities, unified not just by possessing the same
things, such as dogmatic formulas, liturgical rules and
regulations, and hierarchical authorities but, above all, by
sharing the goods of life and their own vitalizing aspirations.
The almost universal call for the establishment of small
communities arises because of their commitment not to
leave the scene of action but to stand on the ground of
real life. Within them mutual recognition and appreciation
within just differences can be established and respect can
be paid and even value given to the individual character of
each person and vocation. To speak of the Church as
building from the ground up would be to risk misunder-
standing, as if primacy were being given to the qualitatively
inferior. Let us say instead that the Church is in process
of remolding some of her features, beginning with a deepening of faith, in "basic communities." The experience of
communion, of Gospel brotherhood, the giving and receiving of all sorts made possible by them is generally a strong,
if not indispensable, support for their members in facing a
world that is more and more often rising from secular and
sometimes inhuman foundations. The whole ecclesial body
is beginning to take on new life because of them.

This experience is accompanied by reflection on "the
local Church," in which the Church as such is truly brought

into being, as Vatican II has already emphasized. Has not Jesus said that where two or three are gathered together in His name He is with them (Mt 18:20)? In its concrete reality, the Church of God continues to abide, not in an organizational system, but in Corinth, Antioch, Rome, Paris, Chicago. . . . God's grace is not suspended somewhere above men's heads but comes to them as they are, where they are, to permeate them and to enter into their diverse situations. It calls them together not to be a herd but to belong to a brotherhood where each individual is invited to become more and more himself and each group, too, is encouraged to seek self-realization.

The Church is not just any kind of a community. It is not even just any kind of Christian community. Certainly Jesus is really present in the midst of those gathered together in His name. But what conditions must we meet to be able to claim that we have come together in His name? In biblical thought a "name" is not just a label, a formality; it expresses the reality of the person or the thing it represents and bears the whole force of the one for whom it stands. To be brought together in the name of Jesus, the name before which ". . . all beings in the heavens, on earth and in the underworld, should bend the knee . . ." (Phil 2:10) is to let ourselves be invested by the whole mystery borne by that name, or at least to consent to remain open to that fullness which no particular community can ever come to equal. The same Church comes into being in Corinth, in Antioch, in Rome, in London and in Calcutta by not closing herself up inside the limits of these particular communities but, while remaining within them, by also continuing to be marked with the seal of God's universal design. The Church, a sacrament of intimate union with God and of unity with all mankind, is realized in and through a diversity of human situations and knows nothing so foreign to its nature as a sect. In Corinth, Antioch, Rome, Manila, and Dar es Salaam any neighborhood or student community is the Church only if it is catholic, that is, universal, in actual relationship, in real and recognizable communion with all the other particular Churches.

The mark of this real and recognizable communion is the hierarchical ministry, a true ministry of unity and universality. A community is the Church only if it is centered in some person whom the other communities as a whole recognize. This they do through their representatives who also have been appointed to stand for them, to draw them together, and to speak in their name. These representatives can be called "heads" if that word signifies rather the head of a body than the dictator of an anonymous mass. The Church is actuated only in the form of a structured community; and her structure is of a kind that lacks the right and power to shape its own form.

In fact, the hierarchical structure not only assures the Church an opening on actual universality, on real and recognizable communion with other communities scattered over the surface of the globe but it also provides the Church of the twentieth century with a bond of communion with the Churches of all times, so that all are together the one Church of Jesus Christ. Surely, here is the deepest meaning of the doctrine called apostolic succession. It is not a matter of a more or less magical transmission of power from its actual custodian to his successor, as a stick is passed from one runner to another in a relay race. In any case, the successor is often installed in office only after the death of his predecessor, so that this is done, not by his predecessor, but by others. The doctrine of the apostolic succession stems from faith not only in the unity but also in the uniqueness of the ministry. It expresses the very simple fact that the Church in a given place can have only one head—since it is a unity and a communion—and that the legitimacy of that head is due to the recognition that is expressed in his consecration and received from the universal Church, the same today, in its continuity, as it has ever been. Recognition by the universal Church is greatly facilitated and even made possible in the concrete by the bond of a common center. The Church at Rome and the successor of Peter, who has presided over it since the beginning, fill that role. The doctrine called the "succession" is fast knit to the affirmation that the Church today, in its historical reality, is quite the apostolic Church, the Church established and sent by Jesus Christ in the beginning.

The hierarchically structured ecclesial community therefore always presents a specific discoverable figure in the midst of all the other human communities. The singular mark that it bears from the time of its origin until its end is also the seal of its radical openness to the universal. It is the confirming testimonial that the coming together at work within the Church, the communion that is being realized there, is free of the limitations that of necessity impose themselves on any group formed as a result of purely human decisions. The Church is a "convocation" by God, according to the primary signification of the biblical term that designates it. The Church cannot then admit of a plan for unity narrower than God's, and His plan embraces the whole human family. The continuing sign of her divine origin represents in some way a constant exigency for expansion and only forbids her to yield to the temptation to be sectarian or partisan. It enlarges to infinity—the very infinity of God—the area opened up for the development of the spiritual life of every believer. Here as elsewhere, God's sign binds only to protect liberty and even to give it greater and greater impetus.[3]

Sacrament

Recalling the hierarchical structure essential for the ecclesial community means that its bond with sacrament has

already been brought to mind. It is by sacramental ordination that bishops and, with them, priests are given the power
of ministry which, especially as exercised in presiding over
the eucharistic assembly, is itself sacramental. In truth, the
whole life of the Church and, in her, the whole faith life
of Christians is informed by sacrament. The sacraments are
preeminent signs of the faith, giving it its Christian or, if
you will, Christly mark. In receiving the seal of baptism the
believer enters into the Christian community and, in it, into
the whole order of God's salvation. In the Eucharist the
mystery of the communion of men with God and of men
with one another within the Church is fast knit and consummated. The other sacraments are in some way organized
in relation to these fundamental sacraments.[4]

As there has already been occasion to note in a general
way, if the Christian faith is really to signify something, it
must of necessity assume some form. However, the sacraments are not just a response to this exigency written into
the constitution of every human reality. For the believer
they have a much more original and really singular signification. In all religions a certain number of rites are to be
found and some of them present an obvious analogy to
Christian sacraments, for example, rites of initiation, sacrificial banquets, and others. Even societies that are officially
most secularized have tended to find for themselves substitutes for religious rites. East Germany offers us a ready
example with ceremonies for the giving of a name, for the
dedication of youth, and for socialist marriage. For this
reason, the singular significance of Christian sacraments is
not sufficiently expressed when we emphasize, as we all
too often do, the necessarily sensible expression of faith
by human beings who are both spirit and body. Christian
sacraments not only conform to the sensible nature of believing man but far more fundamentally, even if these two
aspects are not unconnected, to the historical character of

the faith professed. They are "natural" signs only by being historical signs first. That is what makes them unique. That is the principle of their specificity.

We do indeed find in the sacraments the structures of great natural symbols, such as washing, anointing with oil, taking a meal in fellowship; but these symbols become Christian sacraments only because they have been adopted by a historical gesture of Christ and only insofar as they are actual expressions of his gesture are they sacraments. We must not forget this truth when we are considering possible adaptations of traditional rites in order for them to retain their significant value in different cultural worlds. Should we not, it is asked, celebrate the Eucharist with rice and tea in regions where bread and wine are not a normal part of the diet. This is a legitimate question. The Church has always recognized her own broad authority over what scholastic language terms the "matter" of the sacraments and what we today are more apt to call their form. In what different guises has not the eucharistic celebration been clothed since the first Lord's Supper? Today our ceremonies of baptism are equally distant from baptism by immersion and aspersion. For a certain period, the essential rite of ordination was held to be the porrection, the ordinand's taking into his hands the sacred vessels, the paten and the chalice; but Pope Pius XII, confirming serious studies that had been made on the subject, declared that the essential rite consisted in the imposition of hands. Most of us are familiar with the very different forms that the practice of the sacrament of penance has taken over the course of centuries. It is, therefore, very difficult to define exactly and *a priori* what is absolutely essential to each sacrament. It may even be impossible. A gesture, and what is at issue here is a gesture of Christ, is never reducible to its elements. What is certain is that what we have here is a historical gesture that the Church did not and cannot constitute but does preserve in memory. The sacraments include a memorial element which can never be eliminated and their historical origin, the founding act of Christ, must be recognizable as such.

Surely Jesus settled on gestures as universal as possible to the bearers of salvation to men. What could be more universal than washing, than having a meal with friends? Today we are fortunate in being able to rediscover the way in which the sacraments are rooted in the depths of human reality. But the "natural" symbolism of the sacraments must never lead us to forget their still more fundamental historical signification. It was for the benefit of men that Jesus established the sacraments; and He wanted them, as gestures, to carry such significance that they would reach the very depths of men's humanity. For this reason, we must be careful to see that the sacraments, which in some way actualize these gestures, retain their signifying value within the new cultures where they are introduced and celebrated. We must not forget that they are not only to give expression to the new culture but also to present it with an encounter, also historical, with a different tradition, bringing to it the living and efficient remembrance of a divine initiative proffered precisely in the sacrament.

The sacraments are thus an eminent expression of what is irreducible in the faith. Not that we have to conceive of them as opaque things and rites that prove stumbling blocks in the way of our human faculties and act as a physical force either to do some degree of violence to our intellect and will or work some magic to seduce them.[5] On the contrary, the sacraments come to us to challenge our faith; they speak "a visible word" that translates, without exhausting, a real history ending in a body given and blood poured out—so that we may have the hidden fruits of regenerated life.

Every living word is a sign of transcendence in the sense

that what we say in conversation with another is not offered
as an inert "given" that he can do whatever he likes with
but as a proposition for him to become acquainted with and
to accept or reject. Here is why there is a close kinship and
a bond between the biblical Word of revelation and the
sacraments of the faith. The sacraments attest precisely to
the historical and active character of the Word, which does
not permit itself to be manipulated as if it were a simple
collection of ideas.

Christian faith is, therefore, structured and unified by
the sacraments, which assure it of its singular form. They
also make it impossible for this form ever to fall under the
power of men, whoever they may be, and so preserve it
from ever being reduced to the limitations of human con-
ceptions and purposes. The recent Council thought it very
important to establish the sacramentality of the episcopate.
It emphasized, in fact, that the office of bishop does not
depend just on the juridical structures of the Church and
is not determined only by its organization as a society but
has its foundation first and essentially in the very intervention of God himself. In other words, there is an episcopal
order that preexists all the nominations that a pope can
make and is, in a way, beyond his reach. For this reason,
the apostolic Church is really present, for example, in the
Orthodox Church, although all the jurisdictions exercised
within it may be done independently of any investiture received from the Roman Pontiff. It is equally significant that
baptism, the fundamental sacrament, through which the
Church is continually being established and regenerated,
can be administered by any human being whatsoever, when
he acts according to the mind of the Church. Consequently, there exists a sacramental order and a properly sacramental operation of divine life that reaches beyond the
juridical order and the corporate body of the Church.

We are far from having drawn out all the consequences

that should flow from a sacramental view of the Church. Only within it should juridical determinations be worked out. But the theology and practice of the Roman Church are generally developed as if, on the contrary, the relationship were just the opposite: as if, before becoming a sacrament, the Church first existed as a hierarchical society endowed with certain powers, notably the power of managing the sacraments. This is the reason why, for example, official documents have such difficulty providing a place for the ministry exercised within the separated Orthodox Churches (not to speak of the Protestant Churches). This fact is practically admitted in the *Nota Bene* added to the famous *Nota praevia* of the Second Vatican Council's *Dogmatic Constitution on the Church*. Here we also have the reason why, at the time of the Synod of 1969, in spite of an explicit appeal to the ecclesiology of communion and renewed insistence on the bishops' responsibility for the universal Church in virtue of their collegial aggregation by sacramental consecration, concrete problems were most often dealt with as if, in fact, the sovereign pontiff were the sole principle of unity and authenticity in the apostolic ministry. One of the Fathers had to reintroduce the thought that in the Constitution on the Church and her unity, the Pope as a principle of unity, while surely essential, operates only secondarily, after the Holy Spirit and the Eucharist. How true is it that the juridical standpoint always threatens to absorb the more profound, although not purely interior, viewpoint of the sacramental order.

Well understood, the bond of faith to sacrament prevents the faith not only from having no other basis than itself but also from being defined as a completely social adjunct. From the outset the sacrament establishes faith on the imprescriptible foundation of God's gift to us. He has given us and never stops offering us His own life in Jesus Christ, maintaining it within the infinite reaches disclosed to us in the historical gesture of the Cross.

Canonical Scripture

Christian faith takes its form not only in a structured community and in reference to the sacraments but also in the confession of truth attested in a singular manner within a determined and dogmatically interpreted Scripture.

For a believer, Sacred Scripture is the Word of God by an altogether particular title making it a "canon," a rule of faith. At least at first glance, it is a multiple Word, a Word of many words, with a diversity that for a long time remains irreducible. Then too, it is a Word with limits that appear arbitrary; we know that the boundaries of the Canon were drawn up by a long process in which different factors intervened. But what is significant is that the Church, from the first centuries of her existence, experienced the need to recognize a particular place for the object of her faith. Furthermore, what constituted the singularity of this object for her was not, first of all, the obviously sublime quality of its content (what could be more ordinary in itself than St. Paul's short letter to Philemon?); it was the connection of these writings with the specific manifestation of God accomplished in Jesus Christ. The Church was aware that it was through this singular history, which merged with her origin, that she would continue to rediscover the God who called her together and the mission that He confided to her.

The Church knows that this founding and furthering Word cannot be come upon elsewhere than in the depository of apostolic testimony consigned to Scripture, yet she must always be making a fresh discovery of its true content. Today the necessity to do this seems more imperative than ever, as criticism brings out more clearly than heretofore the complexity of its makeup and the tie between that and the whole historical context within which it is presented to us. By its very activity, exegetical science stimulates us to go beyond the letter of the Scriptures, without, however, breaking away from it, to reach that "spiritual understanding" which believers have always sought. This is what several contemporary exegetes mean when they say that we need "a canon within a canon." They hold that a "discernment of spirits" within Scripture is indispensable. Its principle must not be sought elsewhere than in Scripture itself, which indeed remains the place for the Word of revelation and the canon of faith, called upon at the same time to be ever discovering anew its own content.

Dogmatic Truth

Nonetheless, creativity and a fresh approach are, at least in the Catholic faith, governed by dogma. For many minds today, the tie of faith to dogmatically defined truth is an unsurmountable scandal.[6] It is true that scandal often results from a deficient understanding of the dogmatic reality that binds and structures faith. Too, it is important to comprehend how the dogmatic structure inherent in the faith does not, properly speaking, add to its "scandal" but only gives expression to a particular aspect of its specificity, its constitutive singularity.

Walter Kasper has given us valuable help in refining and deepening our conception of dogmatic reality, first of all, by recalling the semantic and theological evolution that has occurred in this connection.[7] The formal idea of dogma current today is of truth imposed in an authoritarian manner and tied to the faith as a matter of discipline. The concept of dogma understood in this sense is foreign to Scripture and also wears a very different color from that of the whole patristic and medieval traditions. The current idea has spread through the Catholic Church only since the beginning of the eighteenth century and is linked to a particular state of the Church and to a certain understanding that she had of herself in offering resistance to Protestantism and to the rationalism of the Enlightenment. In such circumstances dogma becomes much more a defense of the faith than a quiet and positive formulation of its content. The First Vatican Council, however, while giving full emphasis to the dogmatic character of revealed truth, clearly mentions the principle of the analogy of faith, in virtue of which all propositions must be understood in reference to all the others; and, on the other hand, it insists on the transcendence of the divine mysteries, which are attained even by faith only partially and through a veil.[8] Finally, the Second Vatican Council went beyond the polemical attitude that was the chief characteristic of the period immediately preceding it in the Church's life and did not set out to define "dogmas" properly so called but has provided us with doctrinal teaching of the first importance. Furthermore, it clearly orients us toward an interior and organic conception of dogma, especially in recognizing, within the dogmatic organism, a "hierarchy" determined by the greater or lesser proximity of each dogma to the very center of the mystery of Christian faith.[9]

For the rest, while holding firmly to the indefeasible truth of dogmatic formulas, by taking exception to the relativism which would reduce them to being only attempted and basically inadequate approximations of the reality that they are meant to express, the Catholic Church has also kept the conviction that these formulas have an "intentional" character—this means that the reality to which they are directed is such that they can neither surpass nor exhaust it. A scholastic adage has it: "An article of faith is a perception of a divine truth which tends toward that truth." And St. Thomas has something of the same to say: "Now the act of the believer does not terminate in a proposition, but in a thing,"[10] in the reality designated by the formula.

The historicity of dogma, its tie to the historical existence
of the Church, to the historical status of the faith, is something which, even today, is perhaps less commonly stressed.
Yet, it is by beginning with its historicity, above all, that
we can comprehend the unique and firmly defined form
that dogma gives to faith, at the same time that it opens
up to faith an infinity in which to expand.

A dogma is first an expression of a confession made in
a given context. It is an authoritative word pronounced by
the Church in a definite situation.

> The doctrinal decisions of the Church [Walter Kasper
> writes] always proceed from a situation of a confes-
> sion entirely determined within the history of the
> Church. They are, like every historical reality, con-
> ditioned and relative, not in the sense of being
> deficient but in the positive sense that the Church, in
> her formulation of the Gospel message, is obliged to
> give due attention to the situation and to adapt her-
> self to the law of time.[11]

The law of time, moreover, has already affected the
scriptural text, and there is no apparent reason why it
should deal more leniently with the recovery of its message by the Church. The divine truth that "abides eternally" is always given to us in "an opportune time," in a
kairos, itself founded on "the hour" of every grace, when
God definitely "passed" into the world and the world began to "pass" into God. "Each New Testament writing,"
Kasper writes, "and each dogma attests in its own way for
its own situation to the wholeness of the Gospel."[12] This
is not to take anything away from the permanence of their
truth but only to alert us to the care we should take to
perceive them aright.

Today the faith remains bound by all the dogmatic definitions of the Church and continues to be marked by them. Through them the faith presents a determined, specific form. However, the immutability of doctrine is only one aspect of the Church's infallibility in regard to the faith. If the Church were to deny, even partially, that on which she has pledged her authority and in some way staked her existence, then she would have to admit that she is never sure of what she believes. The divine Word of salvation could only hover above her and her faithful and be at the utmost glimpsed, awaited, and hoped for but not yet given. The Covenant would not be sealed between God and His people. The Church could no longer be truly called the body of Christ, forming one flesh with Him and given life by the indwelling Spirit. All this would mean a departure from the economy of the incarnation.

The existential and historical character of every dogmatic definition, understood as a living confession of faith, also helps us to comprehend how dogma is always not only a destination reached but a starting point as well. In some way, it is a fixed point at which the Church gathers herself together and then uses as a base from which to continue more firmly on her way. Faith must always remain conformed to the definitions that the Church has made throughout the ages. Yet, in its very conformity, faith must not stop seeking to translate its message so that it will really enlighten the people for whom it is destined, in every historical and cultural situation in which they are to be found.

The "development" of dogma, to use Newman's famous phrase, is thus a testimony to the Church's discourse, as she is called upon in every new circumstance to confess the faith received from the apostles and kept indefectibly identical because she remains and wills to remain the same unique Church of Jesus Christ. She preserves the faith exactly in its living identity, not confusing it with the circumstances in which it is expressed in a given epoch and with points of view that these conditions have brought to bear on it, but, on the contrary, by expressing the new relationship that the same immutable truth maintains with circumstances that are ever changing. The development of dogma is not the result of logical deductions from timeless truths. Nor is it solely the organic, progressive development of these basic ideas. It is the expression of a faith lived by the Church in time and in order to enlighten, guide, and save people whose existence is radically bound up with history.

The restoration of dogma in the life of the Church makes it possible to apply to different dogmas the nuanced view that Vatican II recommends to us. While fully engaging her infallible authority in each dogmatic definition, the Church does not always and of necessity pour into each the same amount of the substance of the faith. The points considered are more or less central or more or less peripheral to the mystery of that life by which the faith subsists. Within the Church, it would mean being untrue to the concrete reality of dogma to be capable of apprehending it from the purely juridical viewpoint of the obligation it entails for believers, but not to be equally concerned with the content of mystery which each dogma offers to our believing understanding. These two aspects of a dogma do not always carry the same weight.

Above all, when we recognize how dogma is linked to the historical existence of the Church and to the unique character, the singularity, which must invest all her testimony in the different situations through which she passes, we come to understand how, paradoxically, dogma becomes, for the Catholic faith, the guarantee of its openness and liberty. As a matter of fact, the dogmatic organism is not presented as a system of thought. The faith is rather forbidden to close itself up in any such system, for there is no system of believing life within the Church. In this regard, it is significant that the Church has repeatedly reached a formulation of her faith only by bringing to bear on its inexhaustible object successive points of view: points of view about essence and person in the trinitarian dogmas; points of view on person and natures in the christological dogmas, represented historically by two Councils; points of view regarding primacy and collegiality in the hierarchical constitution of the Church, represented by Vatican Council I and Vatican Council II, respectively. Each time reconciliation seems like a task left to theologians, a task perhaps impossible to accomplish conclusively, if it is true that the faith and life of the Church always exceed any intellectual translation that can be made of them, that they withstand every project to assimilate them into a "gnosis."

Actually, at the same time that the Church binds the faith to certain dogmatic propositions, she refuses to become connected with any theology whatever. Certainly, in the concrete, dogma and theology are closely related. Dogma is obliged to make use of a language normally worked out by theology, and theology can claim to remain Catholic only by allowing itself to be continually confronted by dogmatic statements. However, it is no less important to make a firm distinction between them. While theology builds up from demonstration, explanation, and systematic elaboration, dogma arises from living confession. By its very resistance to systematization, by the variety of its figures, dogma prevents faith from becoming tied to a particular form of thought or a particular spiritual experience. It binds the faith only to the very life of the Church, which transcends all systems and all individual spiritual experiences. Dogma, while providing a firm structure for the faith and assuring it of a specific form, is at the same time the guarantee for its "catholicity," for its continuance in the concrete and essentially living totality of the *Catholica*.

The dogmatic character of the truth of the faith is, there-

fore, not in any way tantamount to an obstacle blocking
the way to thought or preventing research. Of itself it does
not determine any dogmatism, understood as an authoritarian
and more or less unjustified imposition of some inscrutable
thought. Dogma does not hold truth captive. Dogma by
the variety of its aspects only attests to a revelation that is
realized in history in order that there it can be discovered
anew. It furnishes a base of operations for the believer's
understanding and discourse and a sphere which allows for
their true and fruitful development.

Whether it is a matter of the Christian community in the
structures which identify it as such, or of the sacraments by
which faith is seen informed by the very gestures of Christ,
or of the canonical Scripture and of the dogma which
governs the development of faith expressions, everything
that has been said—while trying to keep to essentials—
should suffice to make it clear enough that Christianity is
bound up with certain concrete forms and is, as a result,
always seen in the realm of figures, in the world of signs.
At the same time, these figures all seem to me to open
out upon the universal and to be protective of liberty, even
encouraging the believer to undertake a free and enduring
pursuit of their meaning along ways that remain ever open.

This task properly falls to the believing conscience animated by the Spirit in an experience that I shall try to
describe summarily in the last chapter. It is the believing
conscience, individual and communitarian, which can and
should always continue to rediscover the transparency and
"conductibility" of these figures, to find in them a sustain-
ing and fulfilling means of access to the infinity of God.

CHAPTER 9

Experience under Judgment

The "I" of "I Believe"

A STORY IS TOLD OF AN ENGLISHMAN, FORMED IN HIS country's traditional philosophic empiricism, who decided to have himself instructed in Christian doctrine. The pastor to whom he addressed himself did his best to explain to him the different articles of the Creed. Before admitting his catechumen to baptism, he undertook to ask him for the last time, not only if he understood the different aspects of the doctrine that had been explained, but also if he accepted them without any reservation as to their truth. To each question the candidate answered a wholehearted yes. However, just when the pastor thought that every difficulty had been cleared away and his work finished, his friend said that there was just one little word that had not been explained to him and that it was this precise word that gave him difficulty because he did not see the sense of it: the word "I" in "I believe." What was "I" doing among a lot of truths which merited the name of truth only if they stood up independently of "me"?

Faith as Subjective

This story, probably fictional, presents with a humorous

turn a question that we ought not to pronounce too quickly as silly or stupid. We know that structuralism, at least
some forms of it, undertakes to determine a method of
analysis of human reality which, according to the method
of the natural sciences, would abstract entirely from any
subjective element. For example, language must be studied
without any reference to the speaking subject: "it is said,"
according to the famous formula. What really exists is not
a man who wants to say something to somebody else but a
complex system of signifying and signifieds.

There is no question here of going into the matter of the
interest, the truth, and the limitations of such an approach
to human realities. We would prefer to ask ourselves if
certain presentations of the Christian faith, of the Catholic
faith in particular, are not the effect of the same kind of objectivism. Have we not, on more than one occasion, cul-
tivated the impression that "the Catholic faith" has been
given in a system of propositions established by an authorized magisterium or, in a more concise form, in a catechism
which makes perfectly plain the truths that are to be believed and the duties that are to be performed? A faith of
that nature would be obviously and essentially a monument.

Even if the Reformation, in its own turn, quickly produced a new "system" of truths, we ought to admit that it
has been in part a protest in favor of believing subjectivity.
Luther's sally is well known: "They tell me that Christ is
one Person in two natures! What does that matter as long
as he is my Savior?" And his disciple Melanchton liked
to say, "To know Christ is to know His benefits." Speaking the language of theologians, the *fides qua,* that is, the
attitude of faith, was reevaluated in face of the *fides quae,*
the *object* of faith. For the Reformers, faith is just as much
confidence as affirmation of truth; perhaps it is weighted
even more on the side of confidence. The Bible, with its
existential and certainly not intellectualist orientation, was

to ground and nurture a personalist reaction against a de-
vitalized scholasticism.

In the nineteenth century, one idea came to have the
privilege of restoring value to the personal constitutive element of the faith: the concept of experience. "Religious
experience" became one of the fundamental categories of
the liberal theology then developing in Protestantism. A
little later, it was mentioned quite frequently in Catholic
Modernism. The Catholic magisterium was not alone in
reacting against an inflation of the concept of experience in
faith. Within Protestantism, "dialectical theology," following Barth, submitted the idea of religious experience to
severe criticism, in the name of a faith entirely referred to
the Word of God and to the judgment that the Word brings
to bear on all our experiences as well as on all our enterprises.

Catholic orthodoxy responded with distrust to the positions adopted by Modernism; within Protestantism, dialectical
theology did the same in regard to liberal theology's in-
opportune use of the concept of experience. Both reactions
arose out of fear that the faith would be diluted into human
psychology. There was much apprehension that Christian
faith would be treated like a simple variant of universal
religious experience and so lose its radical singularity, based
on the entirely gratuitous intervention of God, and qualified
by Catholicism as supernatural and by Protestant dialectical
theology as eschatological.

In that decided reaction, another aspect of truth was
easily forgotten or overlooked which both traditions had,
in other circumstances, tended to emphasize. In opposition
to a too extrinsic idea of justification, the Council of Trent
had defined that justification was not "the sole imputation
of the justice of Christ," but that it also consisted in "the
grace and charity which is poured forth in hearts by the
Holy Spirit, and remains in them,"[1] producing authentic

fruits of sanctification. A little earlier in the present work, reference was made to the attention given by the Reformation to the believer's involvement in his faith and to the subjective pole of his relationship with God as defined by that faith.

Protestantism, without necessarily losing all the beneficial aspects of the Barthian reaction, is in process of rediscovering some inalienable intuitions of liberal theology: its sense of the immanence of Christian truth in man and in history, its recognition that, by being immanent in man and in history, Christian truth becomes the proper object of experience. In the Catholic world, certainly one of the objectives of Vatican II was to bring about an actual interiorization of the riches of the faith. What had been too exclusively regarded as a treasure to be preserved was to become light and nourishment for life. We are no longer just to maintain and admire the monuments of the faith but to enter into them. Priests are not to be curators of museums: they have to be "stewards entrusted with the mysteries of God" (1 Cor 4:1). Liturgical reform is particularly significant in this regard, assuming, in all the work undertaken, an exemplary character.

The eucharistic assembly is a privileged representation of the Church and of the exercise of its faith. Now the objective aimed at by reform is that "when the liturgy is celebrated, more is required than the mere observance of the laws governing valid and licit celebration. It is their (the pastors') duty also to ensure that the faithful take part knowingly, actively, and fruitfully."[2] To sum it up, the intention is to have the liturgical mystery move from the sanctuary to the nave and to have the faithful enter into the very heart of the action taking place so that it really becomes their action. Inaugurated by the liturgical reform, the whole work of the Council has consisted in seeking to diffuse the fire of the missionary Spirit of Pentecost throughout the different structures of the Church in order that, being touched in some way by that holy fire, they may regain their suppleness and their capacity to conduct God's grace to God's people.

Here we have the reason why the work begun by Vatican II will never be finished: not only because the structures in question must always be reexamined, always submitted anew to the fire of the Spirit, not to be destroyed by them but to be remolded, but also because within them the movement of life flows on, carried forward by an infinite multiplicity of vocations and charisms. It is a movement of pastoral innovation oriented to greater and greater penetration into the different milieus of life, a movement of intellectual initiative too, aimed at disclosing and "translating" the inexhaustible content of the biblical Word and of Christian dogma. The Dutch Catechism represents one of the efforts made not to be content with just reproducing the contours of Christian truth but to be concerned with drawing out from it its savory and invigorating substance.

A word continues to come to mind in relation to the movement under way because it is expressive of it and at the same time shows the link between the work in progress within the Church and the subject of the present chapter: the word is *experimentation*. In every sphere the need to experiment is felt. Priests and faithful solicit or appropriate the right to do so. For their part, ecclesiastical authorities more and more often deem it necessary that contemplated innovations be first proposed *ad experimentum,* as an experiment. And almost everywhere we can see developing experimental forms of worship, types of communities, and modes of religious life. In the intellectual sphere, perhaps it is more appropriate to speak of "essays" or tentative works but the meaning is the same. It is a question of extending reflection and practice as far as possible so that the realities of the faith will have maximum coincidence with

the human reality, intellectual and existential, that they have
to enlighten and enliven. It is a matter of having the
realities of faith so unite with men's experience that they
themselves become, at least in a certain sense, objects of
experience.

Faith as a Unique Experience

Faith is an experience but, let us say, in a certain sense.
To aim at having the realities of faith become in some way
objects of experience must not lead to vulgarizing them.
Both Catholic orthodoxy in the face of Modernism and
dialectical theology in the face of liberal theology had good
reason to recall the transcendent character of these realities.
If we speak of experience in relation to faith realities, we
ought to insist upon their singular character. In addition,
the concept of experience always needs to be made specific.
We do not, for example, experience a lack, a need, an absence, or again, finitude, as we experience heat and cold.
This reminder is more than necessary today when many
of our contemporaries, especially the young, are so anxious
not to be cut off from experience that they risk understanding it only in the form of the immediate. So they think the
experience of communion can only be real by being felt,
and verified only in the same way. A eucharistic celebration, to their mind, is only authentic when everybody there
knows everybody else and all feel entirely in accord with
one another. As if the Eucharist were meant simply to
put a seal on what has already been realized and not also
intended to make us believe, await, and hope for the impossible. As if one could celebrate the Eucharist while
being sparing with faith.

It is important, therefore, to ask ourselves to what extent
it is possible to speak of experiencing faith. Does not faith
rather require freedom from the limitations of experience in
order to go beyond it?

If we are to speak of an experience of faith, we can never actually insist too much on the unique character, the singularity, of this experience. But why could not being free of limitations, of passing "beyond," constitute, in their own way, an authentic experience? There comes to mind immediately those experiences, themselves paradoxical, of absence, of lack, of need, which both psychology and contemporary literature like to analyze. They present more than an analogy to the experience of faith. Some of their elements are doubtless even an integral part of it. "Negative" theology, as well as the writings of the mystics, has given a telling development of them.

Yet the experience of faith does not come down to an experience of emptiness, of the void, and it is important for us to recognize this. It rests first and more fundamentally on the conviction of the actual reality of the mysterious presence of One whose absence is all the more sensibly felt as it is perceived not as nothing but precisely as the absence of some one. The experience is based on a promise received and still awaiting its complete fulfillment. And so the experience of faith can take the form of nostalgia. Besides, would it be capable of generating action if, through it, nothing were to be expected? The experience of believing is strikingly expressed in the letters of St. Paul, who knew that "to live in the body means to be exiled from the Lord . . ." (2 Cor 5:6; see also Phil 1:23).

The experience of faith, right within the very heart of the negativity which continues to affect it, is then always a qualified experience. Its development within those signs analyzed in the preceding chapter is what maintains its specificity, stamps it with positive meaning and orders it to fruitful action. In the ecclesial community it finds fertile soil; in the sacraments, attestations of the presence of One who supports it in joy and in anguish; in the articulated word of revelation and of dogma, the possibility of being deepened by being spoken. Through these "signs" to which it responds, it is built and renewed over and over again. By their virtue it is enriched even as it is undergoing a process of being at once "emptied" and deepened. For, as has been shown, these signs never stop driving it beyond itself, establishing the existence of the believer deep within an extreme tension which is perhaps one of its most correct expressions. With reason St. Paul could compare Christian life to a race (1 Cor 9:24; cf. Phil 2:16; Heb 12:1). The believer, he again explains, is always at the same time here and elsewhere, thus and otherwise. An infinite distance exists between what he concedes to the usual conditions of existence and what he knows constitutes real life (1 Cor 7:29). Dietrich Bonhoeffer too, when taking a position in opposition to those who believed only in the horizontal dimension of existence, made the statement in one of his letters from prison that he had a special love for the time between Easter and the Ascension because for him it was "an expression of great tension."[3] How, he went on to muse, can the tensions of the world be borne by men who know nothing of the tension between heaven and earth? This tension, lived in the sphere of personal faith, is present in all its dimensions in the eucharistic celebration, in which the Christian community meets the sign of the active presence of its Lord, proclaims His death, celebrates His resurrection, and looks forward to His return in glory. From the beginning, it is in the sacramental liturgy that Christians are conscious of having a surpassing experience of faith.

The Gift of Judgment: "The Sword of the Spirit"

As to liturgical celebration, particularly the celebration of the eucharistic liturgy, here a unique, a singular experience is under consideration. It is an experience of presence, the sensible element of which can be intensified by the whole symbolism of the rites (in the Eucharist most especially by gestures of brotherly communion); but it is a fresh experience too of absence, shown by the sacramental sign itself, referring, as it does, to the person of One who is there "in mystery," or, to put it in another way, in secret, of One who is appealed to and awaited. It is an experience with a recognizable element of the mystical order insofar as our human faculties themselves are endued with the reality celebrated. It is an experience as well of the disproportion between what faith confesses and what indeed we feel and live and are.

It is also an experience of a judgment that overtakes us and to which we submit so that it penetrates us through and through; a judgment which, as far as our experience itself is concerned, "puts it in its place," prevents it from making itself an absolute at the same time that it deepens, supports, and develops it. It is worth remarking that St. Paul associated the idea of judgment and of the discernment that flows from it with his teaching on the Eucharist. After having presented the eucharistic act as "proclaiming the death of the Lord," he goes on to say, "Whoever, therefore, eats the bread and drinks the cup of the Lord in an unworthy manner will be guilty of profaning the body and blood of the Lord. Let a man examine himself, and so eat the bread and drink of the cup. For any one who eats and drinks without discerning the body eats and drinks judgment upon himself" (1 Cor 11:27-29).[4]

In a more general way, the revelation and salvific work of God are presented, from one end of the Bible to the other, in the form of judgment. From that point of view, the Bible does not authorize any simplistic opposition between the existential and juridical. The existential character of Bible thought requires no proof. Neither is there any need to show that the encounter with God that goes echoing throughout the biblical writings did not occur as a kind of "feeling of the divine." It acts more as a definite word that divides the world, the values of life, and even the very being of each man. The word is like a sword, "the sword of the Spirit," as the Epistle to the Ephesians expresses it (6:17). "The word of God is something alive and active: it cuts like any double-edged sword but more finely: it can slip through the place where the soul is divided from the spirit, or joints from the marrow; it can judge the secret emotions and thoughts" (Heb 4:12). The most "spiritual" of the Gospels, St. John's, is, much more than any other, constructed around the theme of judgment, of attack, of discrimination, of division. In His discussion with the Pharisees after the healing of the man born blind, Jesus declares, "It is for judgment that I have come into this world, so that those without sight may see and those with sight turn blind" (Jn 9:39). And the whole Gospel is presented like the unfolding of a dramatic court trial.

Faith is an encounter with and an acknowledgment of God's judgment. It consists in giving ourselves up to that judgment, of placing ourselves "under" it, of letting ourselves be imbued by it, and in being thankful for its mercy. For the judgment of God reinstates man in truth and makes it possible for him, in his turn, to articulate a word of truth. Such is the sense of the Pauline affirmation according to which the believer is "justified" by the "justice" of God (see Rom 3:21-24). The justice of God, far from being contrary to His grace and goodness or even in need of being compensated for by them (it is our idea of God's justice that needs correction), is manifest in His judgment, the very expression of His grace and goodness. His justice is the concrete and active form of His giving.

Still, only faith can recognize the singular nature of God's judgment and of the whole reality it brings into focus. For its manifestation establishes man in a new state, lifts him to a new status. Not that it makes an object out of him, as a certain form of existentialism fears. Before God's judgment, on the contrary, man comes to see himself as eminently responsible in the true sense of the word, not only because, standing before this judgment, he must answer for his actions but because, introduced as he is into the meaning of all things by judgment, he, in turn, becomes capable of judging, of discerning. "A spiritual man, on the other hand, is able to judge the value of everything, and his own value is not to be judged by other men" (1 Cor 2:15), unless it be by the Man who has made him the gift of His Spirit.

The judgment of God becomes the principle of the believer's own judgment. It entirely permeates him and tracks down two "laws" at the depth of his being. "In my inmost self I dearly love God's law, but I can see that my body follows a different law that battles against the law which my reason dictates. This is what makes me a prisoner of that law of sin which lives inside my body" (Rom 7:22-23). Even more than the weight of his fleshly weakness, God's judgment reveals to the believer the fundamental unbelief that urges him without letup to want to develop himself, to construct his own world, to be on his own. From this drive, the Christian can never give up tearing himself free. God's judgment gives drama to his life and brings peace to it too. It alerts him to the abysses that he is skirting: the abyss of despair, of the nihilist temptation; and the abyss of hubris, of wild pride. It deepens his joy in proportion to the very evil from which it delivers him by showing him sin and its wages of death (Rom 6:23).

Structuring and qualifying Christian experience, God's judgment becomes itself experience: the experience of sin and of deliverance. It is an experience that is only in a secondary way negative, for the believer is delivered from his illusory and deadly self-sufficiency only to enter into the positive, actual freedom of God and of His Spirit. He possesses nothing, but everything is his: "the world, life and death, the present and the future . . ." (1 Cor 3:23). Besides, the freedom that he experiences is never an empty liberty but a participation in the creative and liberating work of God that, moment by moment, opens up to us vistas that reach beyond our conception. The encounter with God's judgment in faith leads a man to open himself up to questioning, convinces him that he can be radically free only by letting himself be free, and shows him that his liberty is not a release to destruction and death but an emancipation for affirmation and life.

CONCLUSION

Christian Identity

THE EVER RECURRING TEMPTATION OF THE CONTEMPO-
rary theologies briefly reviewed in the first part of the book
comes in different forms, but basically it consists in stretching to the breaking point the bonds that root Christian faith
in history.

The temptation is not just the fruit of the unbelief that
lurks in the shadows of every believing heart and must be
constantly overcome there; it is also, in some way, part of
the very fiber of the faith itself to the extent that faith is a
provisional state moving toward realization, when all that
has scarred and marred it will disappear (1 Cor 13:10).
Faith is a way to liberty, an initiation into life "in the
Spirit," an entrance through figures into full reality.

As we move forward toward that goal, the human
temptation is to tear ahead, to skip over normal stages of
development, to escape our pilgrim condition and, as a result, to veer off, lose our way, and with it, the good things
to which it leads.

With this human tendency in mind, it seemed useful to
me to reaffirm the organic relationship of Christian faith to
history. History provides the basis for and the determinant
of Christian identity. Faith in this sense is a bond. It ef-

fects "a belonging." By it, the believer accepts being situated.

For the believer, being so situated means only a more resolute search for truth, knowing well the human condition that he shares with other men and realizing, better than most, its limitations. He is aware, too, that all that he possesses of truth is that, in the faith, he can find the fundamental criteria for discernment. For the "figures" that guide his progress and culminate in the figure of Jesus Christ have to be continually reinterpreted. He is always having to discover their true meaning in the Spirit. They continue to be for him what they are in reality only by being perceived as living figures, which challenge him, which keep him both from being satisfied with what he has acquired and from becoming confused, as if he had no way of knowing where he has come from or where he is going. By confronting him continually with the judgment of God, by placing him under that judgment, these figures make it possible for him, in turn, to judge and, far from diminishing his responsibility, they give it foundation and depth. They constantly place him at that point where others have made and where he must continually make the decision which determines each man's destiny.

Christian identity is formed by the indelible relationship of human history to Christian faith, and by the specific kind of presence to everyday life in this world resulting from that relationship.

TITLE: IDENTIFYING CHRISTIANITY

PUBLICATION
DATE: July 1, 1975

PRICE: $4.75

Abbey Press PUBLISHING DIVISION, ST. MEINRAD, IND. 47577

REVIEW COPY

Notes

NOTES TO CHAPTER 1

[1] For a general exposition of Bultmann's thought, reference can be made to the works which I have already devoted to him: *Bultmann et l'Interprétation du Nouveau Testament*, 2nd ed. (Paris: Aubier, 1966); *Bultmann and Christian Faith*, trans. Theodore Dubois (Westminster, Md.: Newman Press, 1967).

[2] Rudolf Bultmann, *Faith and Understanding*, trans. Louise P. Smith (New York: Harper & Row, 1969), vol. 1, p. 237.

[3] See Paul Ricoeur, preface to Rudolf Bultmann, *Jésus* (Paris, Édit. du Seuil, 1968).

[4] Mircea Eliade, *Images and Symbols*, trans. Philip Mairet (New York: Sheed & Ward, 1967), p. 20.

[5] Rudolf Bultmann, *Glauben und Verstehen* (Tübingen, 1952), vol. 2, p. 184.

[6] Henri de Lubac, *Histoire et Esprit* (Paris: Aubier, 1950), p. 381.

NOTES TO CHAPTER 2

[1] The contents of this chapter appeared in part in *Études*, December 1969, pp. 728-738.

[2] Albert Schweitzer, *The Quest of the Historical Jesus*, trans. W. Montgomery (New York: Macmillan, 1968).

[3] Martin Kahler, *The So-called Historical Jesus and the Historic Biblical Christ*, trans. Carl E. Braaten (Philadelphia: Fortress Press, 1964), p. 43.

[4] Rudolf Bultmann, *History of the Synoptic Tradition*, trans. John Marsh (New York: Harper & Row, 1963).

[5] Rudolf Bultmann, *Jesus and the Word*, trans. L. P. Smith and E. H. Lantero (New York: Scribner's, 1958).

[6] Ibid., p. 8.

[7] Rudolf Bultmann, *Theology of the New Testament*, trans. Kendrick Grobel (New York: Scribner's, 1951), p. 3.

[8] Ibid., pp. 26-32.

[9] Ibid., p. 26.

[10] Ernst Käsemann, "Das Problem des historischen Jesus," *Exegetische Versuche und Besinnungen* (Göttingen, 1960), vol. 1, pp. 187-213.

[11] Ibid.

[12] Paul Althaus, *Das sogenannte Kerygma und der historische Jesus* (Gütersloh, 1958).

[13] Ibid., p. 19.

[14] Ibid., pp. 29-30.

[15] Ibid., p. 27.

[16] Ibid.

[17] Joachim Jeremias, *The Problem of the Historical Jesus*, trans. Norman Perrin (Philadelphia: Fortress Press, 1964), pp. 16-17.

[18] Ibid., p. 21.

[19] Heinz Schürmann, "Die vorösterlichen Anfänge der Logientradition. Versuch eines formgeschichtlichen Zugangs zum Leben Jesu," in *Der historische Jesus und der kerygmatische Christus*, ed. H. Ristow and K. Matthiae (Berlin, 1961), pp. 342-370.

[20] Ibid., pp. 369-370.

[21] Ibid., p. 370.

[22] Wolfhart Pannenberg, *Jesus—God and Man*, trans. Lewis Wilkins and Duane Priebe (Philadelphia: Westminster Press, 1968).

[23] Ibid., p. 30.

[24] Ibid., p. 28.

[25] Ibid., p. 23.

[26] Jean de Baroncelli, in *Le Monde*, October 14, 1967.

[27] *Catholic Biblical Quarterly*, 26 (1964), 305-312, and *Dei Verbum*, esp. no. 19.

[28] *Catholicisme* (Paris: Ed. du Cerf, 1938), p. 251 .

[29] Dietrich Bonhoeffer, *Ethics*, trans. Eberhard Bethge (New York: Macmillan, 1965), pp. 130-131.

NOTES TO CHAPTER 3

Translator's note: See James M. Robinson, *The New Hermeneutic* (New York: Harper & Row, 1964), pp. 1-77, for discussion of the use of "hermeneutic" and "hermeneutics." See also Richard E. Palmer, *Hermeneutics* (Evanston: Northwestern Univ. Press, 1969), p. xiv. Robinson suggests that the usage of the singular form may suggest the new turn in the discussion of hermeneutics.

1 For a fuller development, see my work, *Le Problème théologique de l'herméneutique: les grands axes de la recherche contemporaine*, 2nd. ed. (Paris: l'Orante, 1968). Other aspects of the problem can be found in my article "Foi et Interprétation," *Études*, May 1969, pp. 669-682.

2 See especially Henri de Lubac, *The Sources of Revelation* (New York, 1968).

3 Gerhard Ebeling, *The Problem of Historicity*, trans. Grover Foley (Philadelphia: Fortress Press, 1967). See also Ebeling's *Word and Faith*, trans. James W. Leitch (Fortress Press, 1963).

4 Paul Ricoeur, *Freud and Philosophy, an Essay on Interpretation*, trans. Denis Savage (New Haven: Yale Univ. Press, 1970).

5 Ibid., p. 55.
6 Ibid., p. 458.
7 Ibid., p. 459.
8 Ibid., p. 460.
9 Ibid., p. 18.
10 Ibid., p. 497.

NOTES TO CHAPTER 4

1 Much of the content in this chapter has already been included in articles in *Études* (January 1968) and in the review *Lumen Vitae* (1968, no. 3).

2 Friedrich Gogarten, *Despair and Hope for Our Time*, trans. Thomas Wieser (Philadelphia: Pilgrim Press, 1970), p. 83.

3 Ibid., pp. 59-61.

4 Harvey Cox, *The Secular City* (New York: Macmillan, 1965), p. 17.

5 Ibid., pp. 20-21.
6 Ibid., p. 55.
7 Ibid., p. 57.
8 Ibid., p. 58.
9 Ibid., p. 63.
10 Ibid., p. 67.
11 Ibid., p. 68.
12 Ibid., p. 99.

13 Ibid., pp. 77-78.
14 Ibid., p. 127.
15 Ibid., pp. 132-155.
16 Harvey Cox, *On Not Leaving It to the Snake* (New York: Macmillan, 1964), pp. 110-111.
17 Daniel Callahan, ed., *The Secular City Debate* (New York: Macmillan, 1966).
18 Cox, *The Secular City*, p. 67.
19 Ibid., pp. 145, 157.
20 Ibid., p. 161.
21 Karl Barth, *Epistle to the Romans*, trans. Edwyn C. Hoskyns (London: Oxford Univ. Press, 1968).
22 Ibid., pp. 230, 236, 237, 254.
23 Karl Barth, *Church Dogmatics*, ed., Bromiley and Torrance (Edinburgh: Clark, 1956), 1/2, pp. 283-284.
24 Ibid., p. 302.
25 Ibid., p. 327.
26 Ibid., p. 358.
27 Ibid., p. 359.
28 Lesslie Newbigin, *Honest Religion for Secular Man* (Philadelphia: Westminister Press, 1966).
29 Ibid., pp. 36, 38.
30 Ibid., pp. 69-70.
31 Ibid., p. 147.
32 Ibid., p. 148.
33 Ibid., p. 151.
34 Ibid.
35 Ibid., p. 152.
36 For greater detail, see my *Dietrich Bonhoeffer, témoin de Jésus-Christ parmi ses frères*, coll. "Christianisme en mouvement," no. 1 (Tournai-Paris: Casterman, 1967).
37 Dietrich Bonhoeffer, *Letters and Papers from Prison* (London: Fontana Books, 1959), p. 122.
38 Ibid., p. 92.
39 Ibid., p. 123.
40 Ibid., p. 93.
41 Barth, *Church Dogmatics*, 1/2, p. 359.
42 Bonhoeffer, *Letters and Papers from Prison*, p. 166.
43 Ibid., p. 95.
44 Walter M. Abbott, ed., *Pastoral Constitution on the Church in the Modern World* (*Gaudium et Spes*), *The Documents of*

Vatican II (Washington: Guild Press, 1966), no. 19.
[45] *The Documents of Vatican II (Lumen Gentium)*, no. 1.

NOTES TO CHAPTER 5

[1] The material in this chapter has been taken in part from an article in *Études* (November 1968).
[2] Cox, *The Secular City*, p. 259.
[3] Ibid.
[4] James A. T. Robinson, *Exploration into God* (Stanford: Stanford Univ. Press, 1967).
[5] Ibid., p. 45.
[6] Ibid., p. 47.
[7] Thomas Ogletree, *The Death of God Controversy* (Nashville: Abingdon, 1966).

NOTES TO CHAPTER 6

[1] Jürgen Moltmann, *Theology of Hope: On the Ground and the Implications of Christian Eschatology*, trans. James W. Leitch (New York: Harper & Row, 1965).
[2] Ibid., pp. 41, 43, 84.
[3] Ibid., p. 16.
[4] Ibid., p. 17.
[5] Ibid., p. 84.
[6] Ibid., pp. 283-285.
[7] Ibid., pp. 304, 324.
[8] *Der Spiegel*, January 22, 1968.
[9] Ernst Bloch, *Das Prinzip Hoffnung* (Berlin, 1955).
[10] Moltmann, *Theology of Hope*, p. 33.
[11] See Wolfhart Pannenberg, "Heilsgeschehen und Geschichte" in *Kerygma und Dogma*, no. 5 (1959), p. 278.
[12] Heinz Zahrnt, *The Question of God: Protestant Theology in the Twentieth Century*, trans. R. A. Wilson (New York: Harcourt Brace, 1969), p. 201.

NOTES TO CHAPTER 7

[1] Adolf Harnack, *What Is Christianity?* trans. Thomas B. Saunders (London: Williams & Norgate, 1901).
[2] Ibid., pp. 14, 12.
[3] Ibid., p. 17.

4 Ibid., p. 149.

5 Ibid., p. 144.

6 See René Marlé, *Au coeur de la crise moderniste: le dossier inédit d'une controverse* (Paris: Aubier, 1960).

7 This article is reproduced in Ebeling's *Word and Faith* (Philadelphia: Fortress Press, 1963), ch. 1.

8 Henri-Irénée Marrou, *De la connaissance historique* (Paris: Édit. du Seuil, 1954), p. 57.

9 Ibid., p. 153.

10 Oscar Cullman, *Salvation in History*, trans. Sidney G. Sowers (New York: Harper & Row, 1965).

11 Wolfhart Pannenberg, *Revelation as History*, trans. David Graskau (New York: Macmillan, 1968).

12 Dietrich Bonhoeffer, *The Cost of Discipleship*, trans. R. H. Fuller (New York: Macmillan, 1967).

NOTES TO CHAPTER 8

1 This is the dominant idea in Gerhard Von Rad's *Théologie de l'Ancien Testament* (Geneva, 1963-1965). See also Norbert Lohfink, "Sciences bibliques en marche," coll. "Christianisme en mouvement," no. 10 (Tournai-Paris: Casterman, 1969), p. 161 f.

2 *Documents of Vatican II* (*Lumen Gentium*), no. 1.

3 Bonhoeffer offers us some considerations related to this subject. See *Life Together*, trans. John W. Doberstein (New York: Harper & Row, 1954), especially what he has to say about the difference between communities that are "psychic" and those that are "pneumatic" or spiritual, pp. 31-39. Reference can also be made to my *Dietrich Bonhoeffer, témoin de Jésus-Christ parmi ses frères*, pp. 95-98.

4 On this subject see St. Thomas, *Summa Theologica*, III, q. 63, art. 6; q. 65, art. 3; and q. 73, art. 3.

5 We have no intention of going into the medieval discussions concerning the mode of action of the sacraments, whether more or less physical, or more or less moral. Even if they deal with the same question, our considerations belong on a much more elementary level.

6 Some of the ideas presented in the following pages have already been developed under the title "Le Dogme dans la foi," *Études*, January 1967.

7 See Walter Kasper, *Dogme et Evangile*, coll. "Christianisme

en mouvement," no. 4.

8 See *La Foi Catholique* (Paris: Édit. de l'Orante, 1961), nos. 97, 98, 103.

9 *The Documents of Vatican II, Decree on Ecumenism*, no. 11.

10 *Summa Theologica*, II-II, q. 1, art. 3, obj. 2.

11 Kasper, *Dogme et Evangile*, p. 28.

12 Ibid., p. 98.

NOTES TO CHAPTER 9

1 *Canons and Decrees of the Council of Trent*, orig. text and trans. H. J. Schroeder (St. Louis: B. Herder, 1941), Sixth Session, Canon II, p. 43.

2 *Documents of Vatican II, Constitution on the Sacred Liturgy*, no. 11.

3 Bonhoeffer, *Letters and Papers from Prison*, p. 87.

4 This quotation is taken from the Revised Standard Version Common Bible, copyright © 1973, by the Division of Christian Education of the National Council of the Churches of Christ in the U.S.A., and used by permission. All other Scripture quotations are from *The Jerusalem Bible* as indicated on the copyright page.